TRAEGER GRILL

MASTER THE ART OF TRAEGER GRILLING: OVER 1200 DAYS OF MOUTHWATERING RECIPES AND ESSENTIAL TECHNIQUES FOR PERFECT BBQ!

Sonny Greyson

SUMMARY

Chapter 1: Introduction to Traeger Grills 10

What is a Traeger Grill? 10

Why Choose a Traeger Grill? 15

Chapter 2: Getting Started with Your Traeger Grill 16

Unboxing and Assembly 16

Understanding the Basics 19

Chapter 3: Mastering Temperature Control 25

Temperature Settings 25

Troubleshooting Temperature Issues 32

Chapter 4: Essential Grilling Techniques 37

Direct vs. Indirect Cooking 37

Smoke and Sear 38

Chapter 5: Wood Pellets and Flavors 40

Types of Wood Pellets 40

Enhancing Flavor with Pellets 46

Chapter 6: Delicious and Easy Recipes 46

Subchapter 6.1: Beef Recipes 55

Classic Smoked Brisket 55

Perfect Ribeye Steaks 55

Beef Tenderloin Roast 55

Smoked Beef Short Ribs 56

Bacon-Wrapped Filet Mignon 56

Traeger Burgers 56

Beef Tri-Tip 56

Smoked Meatloaf 57

BBQ Beef Ribs 57

Pepper-Crusted Prime Rib 57

Smoked Beef Jerky 57

Korean BBQ Beef Ribs 58

Philly Cheesesteak 58

Beef Brisket Burnt Ends 58

Teriyaki Beef Skewers 58

Subchapter 6.2: Pork Recipes **59**

Pulled Pork 59

Baby Back Ribs 59

Pork Tenderloin 59

Smoked Ham 59

Pork Belly Burnt Ends 60

Stuffed Pork Chops 60

Smoked Pork Shoulder 60

Bacon-Wrapped Pork Loin 60

Honey-Glazed Ham 61

Smoked Sausage 61

BBQ Pork Ribs 61

Pork Carnitas 61

Maple Bacon 62

Smoked Pork Belly 62

Sweet and Spicy Pork Chops 62

Subchapter 6.3: Poultry Recipes **63**

Whole Smoked Chicken 63

Chicken Wings 63

Smoked Turkey Breast 63

Spatchcocked Turkey 63

Chicken Thighs..64

Duck Breast 64

Beer Can Chicken 64

Chicken Kabobs 64

BBQ Chicken Drumsticks 64

Cedar Plank Chicken 65

Smoked Chicken Breast 65

Grilled Quail 65

Stuffed Turkey Breast 65

Smoked Chicken Tacos 65

Herb-Roasted Chicken..66

Subchapter 6.4: Seafood Recipes **66**

Cedar Plank Salmon 66

Smoked Shrimp 66

Grilled Lobster Tails..67

Smoked Trout..67

Grilled Scallops 67

Smoked Crab Legs 67

Grilled Oysters 68

Fish Tacos 68

Smoked Swordfish 68

BBQ Salmon Burgers 68

Grilled Clams..68

Smoked Mahi Mahi 69

Grilled Tuna Steaks 69

Smoked Octopus 69

Garlic Butter Shrimp 69

Subchapter 6.5: Vegetarian Recipes **70**

Grilled Portobello Mushrooms 70

Smoked Stuffed Peppers 70

Grilled Corn on the Cob 70

Smoked Mac and Cheese 70

Grilled Asparagus 71

Smoked Eggplant Parmesan 71

Veggie Skewers 71

Grilled Cauliflower Steaks 71

BBQ Tofu 72

Smoked Sweet Potatoes 72

Grilled Zucchini 72

Smoked Brussels Sprouts 72

Grilled Avocado 72

Stuffed Acorn Squash 73

Smoked Ratatouille 73

Subchapter 6.6: Appetizers and Sides **73**

Jalapeño Poppers 73

Smoked Queso Dip 73

Grilled Bruschetta 74

Smoked Deviled Eggs 74

BBQ Baked Beans 74

Grilled Artichokes 74

Smoked Potato Salad 74

Cornbread 75

BBQ Nachos 75

Grilled Flatbread 75

Smoked Salsa 75

Grilled Stuffed Mushrooms 75

Smoked Guacamole 76

BBQ Corn Fritters 76

Grilled Pita and Hummus 76

Subchapter 6.7: Desserts 76

Smoked Apple Pie 76

Grilled Peaches 77

Smoked Cheesecake 77

Grilled Pineapple 77

Smoked Chocolate Cake 77

BBQ S'mores 78

Smoked Bread Pudding 78

Grilled Banana Split 78

Smoked Brownies 78

Grilled Mango 78

Smoked Pecan Pie 79

Grilled Watermelon 79

Smoked Lemon Bars 79

Grilled Cinnamon Apples 79

Smoked Pears 79

Subchapter 6.8: Sauces and Rubs..**80**

Classic BBQ Sauce 80

Spicy Texas Rub 80

Carolina Mustard Sauce..80

Kansas City BBQ Sauce 80

Memphis Dry Rub 81

Honey Garlic Glaze 81

Smoky Chipotle Sauce 81

Herb Butter Rub 81

Sweet and Spicy BBQ Sauce 82

Apple Cider Vinegar Sauce 82

Cajun Rub 82

Asian Teriyaki Sauce 82

Chapter 7: Advanced Grilling Techniques................................**83**

Smoking Techniques **83**

Using Accessories.. **84**

Chapter 8: Maintenance and Care **85**

Cleaning Your Traeger Grill... **85**

Routine Maintenance **87**

Chapter 9: Sourcing and Preparing Ingredients **90**

Choosing Quality Meat:... **90**

Preparation Techniques **93**

Chapter 10: Overcoming Common Challenges........................... **96**

Time Management **96**

Safety Tips **97**

Chapter 1: Introduction to Traeger Grills

What is a Traeger Grill?

Traeger grills have revolutionized outdoor cooking with their innovative use of wood pellets, which impart a unique smoky flavor while ensuring consistent cooking temperatures. Unlike traditional grills that rely on charcoal or gas, Traeger grills feed wood pellets into a firepot where they burn, generating heat and smoke. This heat and smoke are then circulated throughout the cooking chamber by a fan system, providing even cooking and a distinctive smoky taste. This convection cooking method is a hallmark of Traeger grills.

Traeger offers a variety of models to suit different needs, from portable grills ideal for camping to large units perfect for backyard parties. Features such as digital temperature controllers, meat probes, and spacious cooking surfaces make these grills versatile, allowing for grilling, smoking, baking, roasting, braising, and barbecuing. The range of options ensures that there's a Traeger grill for every occasion and culinary need.

The history of Traeger grills dates back to the 1980s when Joe Traeger sought to address the inconsistencies of traditional grilling. In 1985, he invented the first wood pellet grill, which used an auger system to feed pellets into the firepot and a fan to circulate heat and smoke. This design set the foundation for the modern Traeger grill.

Over the years, Traeger grills have evolved with technological advancements. Early models were straightforward but effective, and as technology progressed, features like digital controllers and Wi-Fi connectivity were introduced. Today's Traeger grills incorporate advanced cooking algorithms and WiFIRE technology, allowing users to control the grill remotely via a smartphone app. This blend of tradition and innovation has cemented Traeger's reputation as an industry leader.

Traeger grills' evolution mirrors trends in outdoor cooking, with a focus on convenience and quality. Their commitment to innovation and user-friendly design has made them a favorite among both amateur and professional cooks. Traeger grills offer a unique cooking experience that combines the rich flavors of wood pellet grilling with modern technology.

The comprehensive range of Traeger grills is designed to cater to different grilling preferences and needs. The portable models, such as the Ranger and Tailgater, are perfect for those who enjoy grilling on the go. These compact units are equipped with all the essential features, including digital controllers and versatile cooking capabilities, making them ideal for camping trips, tailgating events, and small outdoor gatherings. Despite their smaller size, these portable grills do not compromise on performance, delivering the same consistent results as larger models.

For backyard enthusiasts, Traeger offers a variety of larger models that are perfect for home use. The Pro Series, Ironwood Series, and Timberline Series each bring unique features to the table, catering to different levels of grilling expertise and culinary ambitions. The Pro Series, for example, is known for its reliability and ease of use, making it a popular choice for beginners and casual grillers. It includes features like the Pro D2 Controller and WiFIRE technology, which provide precise temperature control and remote monitoring.

The Ironwood Series takes things a step further with advanced features such as the DownDraft Exhaust and TRU Convection systems, which enhance smoke circulation and heat distribution for superior cooking results. The double-wall insulation and Super Smoke Mode also allow for greater temperature stability and enhanced smoke flavor, making it an excellent choice for those who want to elevate their grilling game.

At the top of the range is the Timberline Series, Traeger's flagship line, which offers the ultimate grilling experience. These grills come with all the advanced features of the Ironwood Series, along with additional perks like the Pellet Sensor, which alerts you when pellet levels are low, and the fully insulated construction that maintains consistent temperatures even in cold weather. The Timberline Series is designed for serious grillers who demand the best in performance and versatility.

One of the standout features of Traeger grills is their ability to maintain precise temperatures, which is crucial for successful grilling and smoking. The digital controllers, available on most models, allow users to set their desired temperature with ease, ensuring consistent cooking results every time. The WiFIRE technology takes this a step further by enabling remote control and monitoring through the Traeger app, providing grillers with the convenience of adjusting temperatures, setting timers, and receiving notifications from their smartphones.

The versatility of Traeger grills extends beyond traditional grilling and smoking. With the ability to bake, roast, braise, and barbecue, these grills open up a world of culinary possibilities. Whether you're smoking a brisket, baking a pizza, roasting a chicken, or grilling vegetables, Traeger grills provide the flexibility to experiment with different cooking techniques and recipes.

In addition to their advanced features and versatility, Traeger grills are also designed with user-friendly elements that make grilling more enjoyable and less stressful. The easy-to-clean design, with components like the grease management system and non-stick grill grates, ensures that maintenance is straightforward and hassle-free. The durable construction and high-quality materials used in Traeger grills also guarantee longevity and reliable performance, making them a worthwhile investment for any outdoor cooking enthusiast.

Traeger's commitment to quality and innovation is also reflected in their customer service and support. Traeger offers comprehensive resources, including online tutorials, recipes, and customer support, to help users get the most out of their grills. The Traeger community, which includes a vibrant online presence and various events, provides a platform for grillers to share their experiences, tips, and recipes, fostering a sense of camaraderie and inspiration among Traeger enthusiasts.

The impact of Traeger grills on the outdoor cooking industry cannot be overstated. By introducing wood pellet grilling to a wide audience, Traeger has not only changed the way people grill but also elevated the standards of outdoor cooking. The unique combination of traditional wood-fired flavor and modern technology has set Traeger grills apart from their competitors, establishing them as a leading brand in the market.

In conclusion, Traeger grills have revolutionized outdoor cooking by combining the rich, smoky flavors of wood pellet grilling with innovative features and user-friendly design. From their humble beginnings in the 1980s to their current status as an industry leader, Traeger has consistently pushed the boundaries of what is possible with outdoor cooking. With a wide range of models to suit different needs, advanced features that ensure precise temperature control and versatility, and a commitment to quality and customer support, Traeger grills offer an unparalleled grilling experience that continues to inspire and delight grillers around the world. Whether you're a beginner or a seasoned pro, Traeger grills provide the tools and technology to elevate your outdoor cooking to new heights.

Why Choose a Traeger Grill?

Choosing a Traeger grill means opting for unparalleled flavor, convenience, and versatility. One of the primary benefits of a Traeger grill is the superior flavor it imparts to food. Using wood pellets as fuel, Traeger grills infuse dishes with a rich, smoky taste that is hard to achieve with charcoal or gas grills. Additionally, Traeger grills offer precise temperature control, ensuring consistent results every time. The digital controllers allow for easy temperature adjustments, making it simple to cook a variety of foods to perfection.

Traeger grills are also incredibly versatile. They can grill, smoke, bake, roast, braise, and barbecue, offering multiple cooking options in one appliance. This versatility eliminates the need for multiple cooking devices, saving space and money. The user-friendly design includes features like meat probes, which help monitor internal food temperatures, and WiFIRE technology, allowing remote control via a smartphone app.

Compared to other grills, Traeger grills stand out for their ease of use and consistent performance. Gas grills might heat up faster, but they lack the distinctive smoky flavor that wood pellets provide. Charcoal grills, while offering good flavor, require more effort to maintain consistent temperatures. Traeger grills combine the best of both worlds: the flavor of charcoal grilling with the convenience and precision of gas grilling. This unique combination makes Traeger grills a top choice for both novice and experienced outdoor cooks.

Chapter 2: Getting Started with Your Traeger Grill

Unboxing and Assembly

Unboxing and assembling your Traeger grill is the first step to mastering the art of wood pellet grilling. When you receive your Traeger grill, carefully unpack all components from the box. Ensure you have all the parts listed in the manual before beginning the assembly process. Taking the time to check that all parts are present and in good condition will save you frustration and potential delays later on.

Start by setting up the grill's main body on a flat, stable surface. This could be a patio, deck, or any outdoor area where you plan to do your grilling. Make sure the surface is level to ensure stability and even cooking. If the ground is uneven, consider placing a mat or using leveling blocks to create a flat surface.

Attach the legs to the grill body, ensuring they are secure and stable. Most Traeger models come with detailed assembly instructions that include diagrams to help you through this process. Use the provided screws and tools, or your own, to firmly attach the legs. It's important that the grill stands solidly to avoid any tipping or wobbling during use.

Next, install the heat baffle, grease drip tray, and grill grates according to the instructions. These parts play a crucial role in distributing heat and managing grease, so make sure they are correctly positioned. The heat baffle sits above the firepot and helps to evenly distribute heat across the cooking surface. The grease drip tray catches drippings from the food, directing them away from the firepot to prevent flare-ups and making cleanup easier. Place the grill grates on top, ensuring they fit snugly.

Attach the pellet hopper and auger system, which feeds the wood pellets into the firepot. The hopper is typically mounted on the side of the grill and holds the wood pellets. The auger system is a crucial component that moves the pellets from the hopper to the firepot. Make sure the auger is properly aligned and securely attached to ensure smooth pellet feed. Check the hopper lid to ensure it closes tightly to keep pellets dry and free from moisture.

Once assembled, plug in the grill and fill the hopper with Traeger wood pellets. Traeger offers a variety of wood pellets, each with its own unique flavor profile, so choose the one that best suits the type of food you plan to cook. Common options include hickory, apple, mesquite, and cherry.

Turn on the grill and set it to the initial startup setting as indicated in the manual. This process calibrates the auger and fan system, ensuring even pellet feed and consistent airflow. Allow the grill to run for about 30 minutes, monitoring the temperature to ensure it reaches the specified level. This initial calibration burn removes any residual manufacturing oils and prepares the grill for cooking. During this process, you'll likely see some smoke as the grill burns off these residues. This is normal and part of the process to make sure your food isn't contaminated with any unwanted substances.

While the grill is undergoing its initial burn, take this time to familiarize yourself with the control panel and settings. Modern Traeger grills come equipped with digital controllers that allow you to set precise temperatures and monitor the cooking process. Understanding how to use these controls will make your grilling experience smoother and more enjoyable. If your model includes WiFIRE technology, download the Traeger app and pair it with your grill. This feature allows you to control your grill remotely, monitor temperatures, set timers, and receive notifications, all from your smartphone.

After the initial burn, turn off the grill and let it cool down completely. Once cool, open the grill and inspect the interior to ensure everything looks clean and in place. Wipe down the grates and interior surfaces with a damp cloth to remove any remaining residues from the initial burn. Your Traeger grill is now ready for its first cooking session.

Before you start grilling, it's a good idea to season the grates. This helps to create a non-stick surface and enhances the flavor of your food. To season the grates, brush them with a high-smoke point oil, such as canola or grapeseed oil. Turn the grill to a high temperature, around 450°F, and let it run for about 30 minutes. This will burn off any remaining residues and create a seasoned surface on the grates.

With your Traeger grill fully assembled, calibrated, and seasoned, you're now ready to embark on your grilling adventures. Whether you're a novice or an experienced griller, the versatility and convenience of your Traeger grill will make every cooking session enjoyable and rewarding.

Start with some simple recipes to get a feel for how the grill operates. Grilling burgers, chicken breasts, or vegetables is a great way to familiarize yourself with temperature control and cooking times. As you become more comfortable with your grill, you can experiment with more complex recipes like smoked brisket, ribs, or even baked goods.

Regular maintenance will keep your grill performing at its best. After each use, clean the grates and remove any ash from the firepot. Check the grease management system and empty the drip tray as needed. Periodically inspect the hopper and auger system to ensure they are clean and free from obstructions.

Store your grill in a covered area or use a grill cover to protect it from the elements. Traeger grills are designed to withstand outdoor conditions, but taking these extra steps will help prolong its life and maintain its appearance.

By following these steps and tips, you'll ensure your Traeger grill is properly assembled and maintained, setting the stage for many successful and enjoyable grilling experiences. With your grill ready to go, all that's left is to gather your ingredients, fire it up, and start cooking delicious wood-fired meals that will impress your family and friends.

Understanding the Basics

Understanding the basics of your Traeger grill is essential for achieving optimal results. The grill comprises several key components, each serving a specific function. Familiarizing yourself with these parts and their roles will enhance your grilling experience and ensure you get the most out of your Traeger grill.

The hopper stores the wood pellets, which are fed into the firepot by the auger system. This is where it all begins. The hopper can hold a substantial amount of pellets, allowing for extended cooking times without the need for frequent refills. Different types of wood pellets can be used to impart various flavors to your food. Common options include hickory, apple, mesquite, and cherry, each offering a unique flavor profile. Selecting the right pellets can significantly influence the taste of your grilled dishes.

The auger system is a crucial component that moves the wood pellets from the hopper to the firepot. The speed at which the auger turns determines the rate at which pellets are fed into the firepot, which in turn controls the temperature inside the grill. The auger system is designed to provide a steady supply of pellets, ensuring consistent heat and smoke throughout the cooking process. It's important to periodically check the auger for any obstructions or jams to maintain smooth operation.

The firepot is where the pellets ignite and burn, creating heat and smoke. An electric hot rod in the firepot ignites the pellets, initiating combustion. The firepot's design ensures that the pellets burn efficiently, producing a steady stream of heat and smoke. Proper maintenance of the firepot, including regular cleaning to remove ash and debris, is essential for optimal performance. Ensuring that the firepot is clear of any obstructions will prevent any disruptions in the pellet feeding process and maintain consistent temperatures.

Above the firepot, the heat baffle evenly distributes heat across the grill. This component plays a crucial role in ensuring that heat is evenly dispersed, preventing hot spots and ensuring that food cooks uniformly. The heat baffle also helps direct grease drippings away from the firepot and into the grease management system. Keeping the heat baffle clean and properly positioned is vital for even cooking and preventing flare-ups.

The grease drip tray catches drippings, preventing flare-ups, and the grill grates hold the food. The grease drip tray is angled to direct grease into a bucket or container outside the grill, reducing the risk of flare-ups and making cleanup easier. Regularly emptying and cleaning the grease drip tray is important for safety and maintaining the grill's efficiency. The grill grates, typically made of cast iron or stainless steel, provide a durable and non-stick surface for cooking. Proper care and seasoning of the grill grates will ensure they remain in good condition and provide excellent cooking results.

The control panel is the heart of your Traeger grill's operation. It allows you to set and adjust the temperature with precision. Modern Traeger grills come equipped with a digital controller, which makes temperature management straightforward. The digital controller is easy to use, featuring a temperature dial or buttons to set your desired cooking temperature. The digital display will show the current and target temperatures, allowing you to monitor the grill's progress. The precision offered by the digital controller is one of the key features that set Traeger grills apart from traditional grills, providing consistent and reliable cooking temperatures.

The control panel also features a timer function, which can be set to remind you when to check or turn your food. This feature is particularly useful for longer cooking sessions, helping you keep track of time and ensuring that food is cooked evenly. The timer can be set to alert you at specific intervals, allowing you to focus on other tasks without worrying about overcooking your food.

Additionally, many models include meat probe inputs. By inserting the meat probes into your food and connecting them to the control panel, you can monitor the internal temperature of your meat without opening the lid. This helps maintain a consistent cooking environment and ensures perfectly cooked meals. The meat probes provide real-time temperature readings, allowing you to adjust the grill settings as needed to achieve the desired level of doneness. This feature is especially beneficial for cooking large cuts of meat, such as briskets or whole chickens, where precise temperature control is crucial.

Understanding these components and functions, along with mastering the control panel, will enable you to use your Traeger grill effectively, ensuring delicious and perfectly cooked food every time. The integration of advanced technology and thoughtful design makes Traeger grills user-friendly and highly efficient, even for those new to grilling.

In addition to understanding the basic components, it's important to familiarize yourself with some of the advanced features that Traeger grills offer. One such feature is the WiFIRE technology, available on select models. WiFIRE technology allows you to connect your grill to your home Wi-Fi network and control it remotely using the Traeger app. This feature provides unparalleled convenience, enabling you to monitor and adjust your grill's temperature, set timers, and receive alerts directly from your smartphone. Whether you're entertaining guests or simply relaxing inside, WiFIRE technology ensures you have complete control over your grilling process from anywhere.

Another advanced feature is the Super Smoke mode, which enhances smoke production at lower temperatures. This mode is perfect for achieving an intense smoky flavor in your dishes, particularly when smoking meats like brisket, ribs, or pork shoulder. Activating Super Smoke mode is simple and can be done directly from the control panel or the Traeger app, giving you the flexibility to fine-tune the smoke level to your preference.

Traeger grills also come with a Keep Warm mode, designed to keep your food at serving temperature without overcooking. This feature is especially useful when preparing multiple dishes or waiting for guests to arrive. Simply activate the Keep Warm mode, and your grill will maintain a steady temperature to ensure your food stays warm and ready to serve.

For those who enjoy experimenting with different cooking techniques, Traeger grills offer a variety of accessories that can enhance your grilling experience. Grill mats, smoker tubes, and additional meat probes are just a few examples of the accessories available. Grill mats provide a non-stick surface for cooking delicate items like fish or vegetables, while smoker tubes allow you to add extra smoke flavor to your food. Additional meat probes can be used to monitor multiple pieces of meat simultaneously, ensuring each one is cooked to perfection.

Maintaining your Traeger grill is also straightforward, thanks to its user-friendly design. Regular cleaning and maintenance are essential to keep your grill in top condition and ensure it performs optimally. Start by cleaning the grill grates after each use to remove any food residue and prevent buildup. Empty and clean the grease drip tray regularly to avoid flare-ups and maintain a clean cooking environment. Periodically check the hopper and auger system for any obstructions or pellet dust, and clean them as needed to ensure smooth operation.

Understanding the basics of your Traeger grill and familiarizing yourself with its advanced features and accessories will allow you to fully harness its potential. Whether you're grilling, smoking, baking, roasting, braising, or barbecuing, your Traeger grill provides the tools and technology to achieve delicious and perfectly cooked food every time. By mastering the components and functions of your grill, you can elevate your outdoor cooking experience and impress your family and friends with mouthwatering dishes.

Chapter 3: Mastering Temperature Control

Temperature Settings

Mastering temperature control is crucial for getting the most out of your Traeger grill. The ability to set and maintain precise temperatures sets Traeger grills apart from traditional grilling methods. Traeger grills offer a range of temperature settings, from low to high, which accommodate various cooking techniques such as smoking, roasting, and grilling. This versatility allows you to cook a wide variety of foods to perfection, whether you are slow-smoking a brisket or searing a steak.

To set and adjust the temperature, start by turning on the grill and using the control panel to select your desired cooking temperature. Modern Traeger grills feature digital controllers that allow you to adjust the temperature in small increments, providing greater control over the cooking process. Simply turn the dial or use the buttons to set the desired temperature, and the grill will automatically maintain it by regulating the pellet feed and fan speed. This precise temperature control is essential for achieving consistent and repeatable results, making it easier to follow recipes and produce high-quality dishes.

Understanding temperature zones within your grill is also essential. The grill's cooking surface can have different heat zones, typically hotter near the firepot and cooler towards the edges. Recognizing these zones helps in cooking different types of food simultaneously. For instance, you can place thicker cuts of meat or items that require higher temperatures directly over the firepot, while more delicate foods can be positioned towards the outer edges. This technique allows you to cook multiple dishes at once, maximizing the efficiency of your grill and ensuring that everything is ready to serve at the same time.

The ability to maintain consistent temperatures is particularly important when smoking, as this cooking method relies on low and slow heat to break down tough connective tissues and render fat. For smoking, you'll typically set your Traeger grill to a lower temperature range, such as 180°F to 225°F. This gentle heat allows the smoke to penetrate the meat deeply, infusing it with rich, smoky flavors over several hours. To achieve the best results, monitor the internal temperature of the meat using a meat probe and adjust the grill's temperature as needed to maintain a steady heat.

When roasting, you'll want to use a moderate temperature range, usually between 300°F and 375°F. This method is ideal for cooking whole poultry, large cuts of beef, or pork roasts. The even heat distribution provided by the Traeger grill ensures that the meat cooks uniformly, with a beautifully browned exterior and juicy interior. To enhance the flavor, consider using a dry rub or marinade, and baste the meat periodically with its own juices or a flavorful glaze.

Grilling typically requires higher temperatures, ranging from 400°F to 500°F. This high heat is perfect for searing steaks, burgers, and vegetables, creating a delicious caramelized crust while keeping the inside tender and moist. To achieve the perfect sear, preheat your Traeger grill to the desired temperature and place the food directly over the firepot. Sear each side for a few minutes until a crust forms, then move the food to a cooler zone to finish cooking if necessary. This two-zone cooking method ensures that the food is cooked to the desired level of doneness without burning the exterior.

In addition to understanding the basic temperature settings, it's important to familiarize yourself with the advanced features that Traeger grills offer for temperature control. One such feature is the Super Smoke mode, available on select models. This mode enhances smoke production at lower temperatures, typically between 165°F and 225°F, which is ideal for adding an intense smoky flavor to your food. Activating Super Smoke mode is simple and can be done directly from the control panel or the Traeger app, giving you the flexibility to fine-tune the smoke level to your preference.

Another useful feature is the Keep Warm mode, which maintains your food at serving temperature without overcooking. This feature is especially handy when you're preparing multiple dishes or waiting for guests to arrive. Simply activate the Keep Warm mode, and your grill will maintain a steady temperature to ensure your food stays warm and ready to serve.

For those who enjoy experimenting with different cooking techniques, Traeger grills offer a variety of accessories that can enhance your temperature control capabilities. Grill mats, smoker tubes, and additional meat probes are just a few examples of the accessories available. Grill mats provide a non-stick surface for cooking delicate items like fish or vegetables, while smoker tubes allow you to add extra smoke flavor to your food. Additional meat probes can be used to monitor multiple pieces of meat simultaneously, ensuring each one is cooked to perfection.

Maintaining your Traeger grill is also essential for optimal temperature control. Regular cleaning and maintenance help ensure that the grill operates efficiently and that the temperature settings remain accurate. Start by cleaning the grill grates after each use to remove any food residue and prevent buildup. Empty and clean the grease drip tray regularly to avoid flare-ups and maintain a clean cooking environment. Periodically check the hopper and auger system for any obstructions or pellet dust, and clean them as needed to ensure smooth operation.

Understanding and mastering temperature control on your Traeger grill will allow you to fully harness its potential, making every meal a success. Whether you're a novice griller or a seasoned pro, the ability to set and maintain precise temperatures is key to producing consistently delicious food. With the advanced features and user-friendly design of Traeger grills, you can achieve professional-level results with ease.

In addition to the practical aspects of temperature control, it's also worth exploring the science behind it. The Maillard reaction, for example, is a chemical process that occurs when proteins and sugars in food are exposed to high heat, resulting in the development of complex flavors and aromas. This reaction is responsible for the savory, caramelized crust on grilled meats and vegetables. By understanding how temperature affects the Maillard reaction, you can better control the cooking process to achieve the desired flavor profile.

Another important concept is the smoke ring, a pink layer found just beneath the surface of smoked meats. This ring is formed when nitrogen dioxide in the smoke reacts with the myoglobin in the meat. To achieve a pronounced smoke ring, it's important to maintain a low and steady temperature, allowing the meat to absorb the smoke over an extended period. The presence of a smoke ring is often seen as a mark of well-executed smoking, adding both visual appeal and a deeper smoky flavor to the meat.

Water pan usage is another technique that can aid in temperature control, especially during long smoking sessions. Placing a pan of water in the grill helps to stabilize the temperature and adds moisture to the cooking environment, preventing the meat from drying out. The steam produced by the water pan can also help distribute heat more evenly across the cooking surface, ensuring that all parts of the meat are cooked uniformly.

Mastering temperature control also involves understanding how different types of wood pellets affect the cooking process. Hardwood pellets burn at different rates and produce varying levels of heat and smoke. For instance, oak pellets burn hotter and longer, making them ideal for high-temperature grilling and roasting. Fruitwood pellets, such as apple and cherry, produce a milder smoke and are well-suited for smoking delicate meats like poultry and fish. By experimenting with different wood pellets, you can fine-tune the flavor and temperature to match your specific culinary goals.

Altitude and weather conditions can also impact temperature control. At higher altitudes, the air is thinner, which can affect the combustion process and the grill's ability to maintain consistent temperatures. Similarly, cold or windy weather can influence heat retention and distribution. Understanding how to adjust your grill settings to account for these factors will help you achieve consistent results regardless of external conditions.

For advanced users, investing in a thermal blanket or insulation cover can improve temperature stability in extreme weather conditions. These accessories help retain heat and reduce pellet consumption, making it easier to maintain the desired temperature even in cold or windy environments.

In conclusion, mastering temperature control on your Traeger grill is essential for achieving the best possible results. By understanding the grill's temperature settings, recognizing heat zones, and utilizing advanced features and accessories, you can cook a wide variety of foods to perfection. Regular maintenance and a solid grasp of the science behind temperature control will further enhance your grilling experience, allowing you to produce consistently delicious and visually appealing dishes. Whether you're smoking, roasting, or grilling, the precision and versatility of your Traeger grill will help you elevate your outdoor cooking to new heights.

Troubleshooting Temperature Issues

combustion and heat consistency. Inferior pellets can produce excessive ash, uneven burn rates, and unpredictable temperatures, leading to inconsistent cooking results. It's also essential to store pellets properly in a dry, cool place to prevent moisture absorption, which can affect their performance.

Another issue might be the grill not reaching the set temperature. This can happen if the firepot is clogged with ash or if there is an obstruction in the auger system. Regularly clean the firepot and ensure the auger is free of blockages. A clean firepot allows for proper airflow and efficient pellet combustion, which is critical for reaching and maintaining the desired temperature. If the grill is still not heating properly, check for a damaged or worn-out hot rod, which ignites the pellets. Replacing the hot rod might be necessary if it's not functioning correctly. The hot rod is a vital component that ensures the pellets ignite properly to produce the necessary heat and smoke.

Maintaining consistent heat is crucial for achieving perfect cooking results. To do this, ensure the pellet hopper is always adequately filled, as running out of pellets can cause temperature drops. An empty hopper means the grill cannot feed pellets into the firepot, causing the temperature to drop quickly. Regularly check the pellet levels during long cooking sessions to avoid this issue. Investing in a pellet sensor can help monitor pellet levels more effectively, providing alerts when the hopper needs refilling.

Regularly clean the grill, especially the heat baffle and drip tray, to prevent grease buildup, which can affect heat distribution. Grease buildup can not only cause flare-ups but also obstruct heat flow, leading to uneven cooking. A clean grill ensures that heat circulates efficiently and that grease and debris do not interfere with the temperature control. Additionally, avoid frequently opening the grill lid, as this causes heat to escape and can lead to temperature fluctuations. Each time the lid is opened, the internal temperature drops, and the grill needs time to recover to the set temperature, affecting the cooking process.

To further stabilize temperatures, consider using a thermal blanket, especially in colder climates. A thermal blanket helps insulate the grill, retaining heat and reducing pellet consumption by minimizing the effects of external temperature changes. This can be particularly beneficial for long smoking sessions or during the winter months when maintaining a steady temperature is more challenging.

Another common temperature issue is the grill taking too long to heat up. This can be caused by a few factors, including cold weather, high humidity, or a full grease drip tray. In cold weather, preheating the grill can take longer as the external temperature cools the grill down. To mitigate this, preheat the grill with the lid closed and allow extra time for the grill to reach the desired temperature. High humidity can also affect the grill's performance by making it harder for the pellets to ignite and burn efficiently. Ensure the pellets are dry before using them to prevent this issue.

If the grill's temperature is still unstable, checking the P-setting can be crucial. The P-setting controls the interval at which pellets are fed into the firepot. Adjusting this setting can help stabilize the temperature by ensuring a consistent pellet feed rate. For example, in colder weather or at higher altitudes, you might need to increase the P-setting to provide more pellets and maintain the desired temperature. Conversely, in warmer conditions, you might need to decrease the P-setting to prevent overshooting the temperature.

Additionally, regularly inspect the grill's seals and gaskets to ensure they are intact and providing a proper seal. Damaged or worn-out gaskets can allow heat and smoke to escape, leading to temperature fluctuations and inefficient cooking. Replacing these components when necessary will help maintain the grill's efficiency and temperature stability.

The positioning of the meat probes is also crucial for accurate temperature readings. Ensure the probes are inserted into the thickest part of the meat, away from bones and fat pockets, to get an accurate internal temperature. Proper probe placement helps ensure the meat is cooked evenly and prevents undercooking or overcooking.

For those experiencing persistent temperature issues, it may be helpful to recalibrate the grill. Recalibrating the temperature controller can sometimes resolve inconsistencies by resetting the system to its factory settings. Refer to the user manual for specific instructions on how to perform this recalibration process.

Another advanced troubleshooting step is to check the auger motor and fan. The auger motor should turn smoothly and consistently, feeding pellets into the firepot at a steady rate. If the motor is making unusual noises or seems to be struggling, it may need to be cleaned or replaced. The fan should also operate without obstruction, ensuring proper airflow through the grill. Any blockages or malfunctions in these components can lead to temperature issues.

Understanding the impact of external factors, such as altitude and weather, on grilling performance is also important. At higher altitudes, the air pressure is lower, which can affect combustion and temperature stability. Adjusting the grill's settings and allowing extra time for preheating can help mitigate these effects. Similarly, during windy conditions, placing the grill in a sheltered location or using windbreaks can prevent the wind from disrupting the temperature.

Lastly, engaging with the Traeger community can provide valuable insights and tips for troubleshooting temperature issues. Online forums, social media groups, and Traeger's official support channels offer a wealth of information from experienced users and experts. Sharing your experiences and learning from others can help identify solutions to common problems and improve your overall grilling skills.

By addressing these common problems and following these tips, you can maintain consistent heat in your Traeger grill, ensuring reliable and delicious cooking outcomes every time. Understanding how to troubleshoot and maintain your grill will enhance your grilling experience and help you achieve perfect results with every use. Regular maintenance, proper cleaning, and understanding the nuances of your grill's operation are key to enjoying the full benefits of your Traeger grill. Whether you're a seasoned griller or a beginner, mastering these troubleshooting techniques will ensure you can tackle any temperature issue with confidence and continue to produce mouthwatering dishes for years to come.

In summary, troubleshooting temperature issues on your Traeger grill involves a combination of proper maintenance, understanding the grill's components, and adjusting settings to suit external conditions. Regularly cleaning the firepot, checking the auger system, using high-quality pellets, and ensuring the grill is sheltered from wind are essential steps in maintaining consistent temperatures. Additionally, understanding and utilizing advanced features like the P-setting, thermal blankets, and proper probe placement can further enhance temperature stability. By mastering these techniques and engaging with the Traeger community for additional support, you can ensure your grill performs optimally, delivering delicious and consistent results every time.

Chapter 4: Essential Grilling Techniques

Direct vs. Indirect Cooking

Understanding essential grilling techniques is key to maximizing the versatility and performance of your Traeger grill. Two primary methods you'll use are direct and indirect cooking. Each technique serves different purposes and knowing when and how to use them can significantly impact your grilling results.

Direct cooking involves placing food directly over the heat source, making it ideal for searing and cooking items that require high heat for short periods. Examples include steaks, burgers, and vegetables. To achieve the best results with direct cooking on your Traeger grill, preheat the grill to a high temperature and place the food directly over the firepot. This method ensures a quick, flavorful sear, locking in juices and creating a delicious crust.

Indirect cooking, on the other hand, positions food away from the direct heat source, utilizing the grill's convection capabilities. This technique is perfect for larger cuts of meat or dishes that require slow, even cooking, such as roasts, whole chickens, and ribs. To utilize indirect cooking, preheat the grill to a lower temperature and place the food on the grill grates away from the firepot, allowing the heat and smoke to circulate around the food evenly.

Best practices for these methods include understanding the appropriate temperature settings and using a meat thermometer to monitor internal temperatures. Direct cooking is best for foods needing a high heat blast, while indirect cooking is ideal for slow-cooked, tender results. By mastering both techniques, you can enhance the flavor and texture of your dishes, ensuring perfect grilling outcomes every time.

Smoke and Sear

Achieving the perfect smoke ring and mastering searing techniques are essential skills for elevating your grilling game with a Traeger grill. Smoke rings, the coveted pink layers just beneath the surface of smoked meats, are a sign of well-executed smoking. They form when nitrogen dioxide from wood smoke reacts with the meat's myoglobin. To create a perfect smoke ring, start by using high-quality wood pellets, as they produce consistent, clean smoke. Preheat your Traeger grill to a low temperature, around 225°F, to encourage a longer exposure to smoke. Ensure the meat is cold when it goes on the grill; this extends the time it takes to reach the surface temperature where the smoke ring forms.

Searing is another technique that enhances flavor and texture. It involves cooking the surface of the meat at high temperatures to create a caramelized crust. This crust, rich in Maillard reaction flavors, contrasts with the tender, juicy interior. To sear on a Traeger grill, preheat the grill to its highest setting. Use the grill grates directly above the firepot for maximum heat exposure. Pat the meat dry before placing it on the grill to prevent steaming, and sear each side for a few minutes until a dark, flavorful crust develops.

Combining smoking and searing techniques can produce exceptional results. Smoke the meat at a low temperature to develop a smoke ring and infuse it with flavor, then finish with a high-heat sear to create a crusty exterior. This method, often called "reverse searing," provides the best of both worlds: deep smoky flavor and a perfect sear. Mastering these techniques will help you make the most of your Traeger grill, resulting in dishes that are both visually impressive and deliciously flavorful.

Chapter 5: Wood Pellets and Flavors

Types of Wood Pellets

Wood pellets are the heart of your Traeger grill, imparting distinctive flavors that elevate your cooking. Understanding the different types of wood pellets and how to choose the right one for your recipe is crucial for achieving the best results. Traeger offers a variety of wood pellets, each with unique flavor profiles. The most popular types include hickory, mesquite, apple, cherry, and oak. Each type of pellet brings a different taste to the table, enhancing the natural flavors of the food you're cooking and allowing you to tailor your grilling experience to your preferences.

Hickory pellets are known for their strong, smoky flavor, making them ideal for beef and pork. This type of wood pellet provides a robust, bacon-like smoke that complements the rich flavors of meats such as ribs, brisket, and pork shoulders. The intense smoke flavor penetrates deeply into the meat, creating a savory taste that is highly desirable for traditional barbecue dishes.

Mesquite pellets provide an intense, earthy taste, perfect for grilling meats with bold flavors. Mesquite is one of the strongest-flavored wood pellets, delivering a powerful punch that pairs well with beef, especially steaks and burgers. The hearty smoke of mesquite is also excellent for game meats like venison and lamb, adding a distinctive southwestern flair to your dishes.

Apple pellets offer a mild, fruity flavor that pairs well with poultry and pork. The sweetness of apple wood enhances the natural flavors of chicken, turkey, and pork loin, giving them a delicate, fragrant smoke. Apple pellets are also a great choice for smoking cheese and vegetables, where a subtle smoke flavor is preferred over stronger options.

Cherry pellets deliver a sweet, subtle smoke suitable for all meats and even vegetables. The slightly fruity and sweet aroma of cherry wood adds a beautiful reddish hue to meats, making it a favorite for smoking ribs, chicken, and ham. The mild smoke flavor from cherry pellets is versatile enough to complement seafood and vegetables, providing a delightful and nuanced taste.

Oak pellets are versatile, offering a balanced smoke flavor that complements a wide range of foods. Oak is a hardwood that burns hot and steady, making it ideal for both low-and-slow smoking and high-heat grilling. The moderate smokiness of oak works well with all types of meats, poultry, and vegetables, making it a reliable choice for any recipe.

Choosing the right pellets depends on the type of food you're cooking and the flavor profile you want to achieve. For a robust, smoky taste, use hickory or mesquite. If you prefer a sweeter, milder smoke, opt for apple or cherry pellets. Oak is a great all-purpose choice that works well with most recipes. The key is to match the wood pellet to the meat or dish you are preparing to enhance the flavors without overpowering them.

Experimenting with different pellet types and combinations can also enhance your dishes. Mixing pellets allows you to create custom flavor profiles tailored to your preferences. For instance, combining hickory and cherry pellets can provide a balanced smoke with a hint of sweetness, perfect for pork ribs or chicken. You might also try blending apple and oak pellets for a subtle, yet robust flavor that works well with turkey or fish. The possibilities are endless, and experimenting with different combinations can lead to unique and delicious results.

By understanding the characteristics of different wood pellets and how to pair them with various foods, you can unlock the full potential of your Traeger grill and create mouthwatering, flavor-rich dishes every time you cook. Here are some additional insights and tips to help you make the most out of your wood pellet selections:

Storage and Handling of Wood Pellets

Proper storage and handling of wood pellets are essential to maintain their quality and performance. Wood pellets are hygroscopic, meaning they can absorb moisture from the air, which can affect their ability to burn efficiently and produce smoke. To prevent this, store your pellets in a cool, dry place, preferably in an airtight container or a specially designed pellet storage bin. Keeping pellets dry ensures they burn consistently, providing the steady heat and smoke necessary for optimal grilling and smoking.

Understanding Smoke Intensity and Duration

Different types of wood pellets not only offer unique flavors but also vary in their intensity and burn duration. For instance, mesquite and hickory pellets produce a strong, dense smoke that infuses food quickly, making them ideal for shorter cooking times or when a bold smoke flavor is desired. On the other hand, apple and cherry pellets generate a lighter, sweeter smoke that can be used for longer cooking sessions without overwhelming the food. Oak pellets fall somewhere in between, offering a moderate smoke intensity suitable for a wide range of cooking times and styles.

Pairing Wood Pellets with Specific Foods

When selecting wood pellets, consider the type of food you plan to cook and the flavor profile you wish to achieve:

Beef: Stronger woods like hickory, mesquite, or oak work best with beef. These woods complement the rich, hearty flavors of steaks, brisket, and ribs, providing a robust smoky taste that enhances the natural beefiness.

Pork: Apple, cherry, and hickory pellets are excellent choices for pork. Apple and cherry add a sweet, fruity undertone that pairs well with pork's mild flavor, while hickory provides a more traditional, smoky barbecue flavor.

Poultry: Apple, cherry, and oak are great for chicken and turkey. The mild smoke from apple and cherry enhances poultry without overpowering it, and oak provides a balanced, versatile smoke.

Seafood: Milder woods like apple, cherry, or a blend of apple and oak are ideal for seafood. These woods impart a subtle flavor that complements the delicate taste of fish and shellfish.

Vegetables: Apple and cherry pellets add a sweet, light smoke to vegetables, enhancing their natural flavors without being too intense. Oak can also be used for a more robust smoky taste.

Creating Custom Blends

One of the joys of using a Traeger grill is the ability to experiment with custom pellet blends to create unique flavors. Start with a base wood that complements the main ingredient of your dish and then add another wood to introduce new flavor notes. For example, if you're smoking a pork shoulder, you might use a base of hickory for its strong smoke flavor and add apple pellets for a touch of sweetness. Similarly, for grilled chicken, you could blend oak and cherry pellets to balance a rich, smoky flavor with a hint of fruitiness.

Experimenting with Different Cooking Techniques

Wood pellets aren't just for smoking. They can also be used for grilling, roasting, and baking on your Traeger grill. Experimenting with different cooking techniques and pellet types can yield exciting and delicious results:

Grilling: Use higher heat and quicker cooking times with pellets like mesquite or hickory to achieve a rich, charred flavor on steaks, burgers, and chops.
Roasting: Combine oak pellets with fruitwood pellets like apple or cherry to roast poultry, pork, or vegetables, creating a balanced, flavorful crust and tender interior.
Baking: Wood pellets can add a unique twist to baked goods. Try using apple or cherry pellets to bake pies, bread, or even cookies, infusing them with a subtle smoky sweetness.
Sustainability and Quality Assurance

Traeger's wood pellets are made from 100% natural hardwood, ensuring a clean burn and pure smoke flavor without additives or fillers. Choosing high-quality pellets is not only crucial for flavor but also for the longevity and performance of your grill. Traeger's commitment to sustainability means their pellets are sourced from responsibly managed forests, providing an eco-friendly option for your grilling needs.

Maximizing Smoke Absorption

For the best smoke absorption, use the Traeger grill's Super Smoke mode if available. This feature increases the smoke output at lower temperatures, perfect for infusing meats with a deep, smoky flavor. Additionally, try to keep the grill lid closed as much as possible during cooking to maintain a steady flow of smoke and consistent temperature.

Seasonal Considerations

Different seasons can affect how your grill and pellets perform. In colder months, preheat your grill longer and consider using a thermal blanket to help maintain temperature and reduce pellet consumption. During humid conditions, ensure your pellets are dry to prevent difficulties in maintaining a steady burn.

By mastering the use of different wood pellets and understanding how to pair them with various foods, you can unlock the full potential of your Traeger grill. Each type of pellet brings its own unique flavor profile, and experimenting with different combinations allows you to customize your grilling experience to your tastes. Proper storage, handling, and understanding the nuances of each wood type will ensure consistently delicious and flavorful dishes, making every grilling session a culinary adventure. With Traeger wood pellets, you can elevate your outdoor cooking to new heights, creating memorable meals for family and friends.

Enhancing Flavor with Pellets

Enhancing flavor with wood pellets is one of the most exciting aspects of using a Traeger grill. Each type of wood pellet has a distinct flavor profile that can significantly influence the taste of your food. Hickory and mesquite pellets are known for their strong, bold flavors. Hickory provides a hearty smoke that pairs well with beef, pork, and game meats, while mesquite offers an intense, earthy flavor, ideal for grilling robust meats like brisket and ribs.

For those seeking a milder smoke, fruitwood pellets such as apple and cherry are excellent choices. Apple pellets impart a sweet, light smoke that complements pork, poultry, and even baked goods. Cherry pellets deliver a slightly tart yet sweet smoke, adding depth to chicken, turkey, and vegetables. Oak pellets offer a medium smoke flavor that is versatile and works well with almost any type of food, providing a balanced, subtle smokiness without overpowering the dish.

Mixing and matching pellets allows you to create unique flavor profiles tailored to your tastes. Combining hickory and apple pellets, for instance, can give you a robust, smoky flavor with a hint of sweetness, perfect for pork ribs. Mixing cherry and oak pellets can offer a balanced smoke that enhances both meat and vegetables.

Experimenting with different pellet combinations can lead to discovering new favorite flavors. Try blending mesquite with fruitwoods for a bold yet nuanced smoke, or mix oak with a touch of cherry for a well-rounded flavor. By understanding the flavor profiles of various woods and how they interact, you can enhance the taste of your dishes, making every meal on your Traeger grill a culinary adventure.

Wood Pellet Flavors and Their Best Uses

Hickory Pellets:

Flavor Profile: Strong, smoky, bacon-like.

Best Uses: Beef, pork, ribs, brisket, game meats.

Description: Hickory pellets produce a robust and hearty smoke that deeply penetrates the meat, making them ideal for long, slow-cooking processes like smoking. The strong smoke flavor pairs exceptionally well with the rich, savory taste of beef and pork, enhancing their natural flavors and adding a delicious smoky crust.

Mesquite Pellets:

Flavor Profile: Intense, earthy, bold.

Best Uses: Beef, brisket, ribs, lamb, game meats.

Description: Mesquite is known for its powerful, earthy smoke that can stand up to and enhance the flavors of the most robust meats. It is particularly well-suited for grilling steaks, brisket, and ribs, providing a distinctive southwestern taste. Mesquite can be quite potent, so it's often best used in moderation or blended with milder woods.

Apple Pellets:

Flavor Profile: Sweet, fruity, mild.

Best Uses: Pork, poultry, seafood, baked goods.

Description: Apple pellets offer a gentle, sweet smoke that pairs beautifully with lighter meats like pork and poultry. The subtle fruity notes add complexity to the meat without overwhelming its natural flavors. Apple wood is also excellent for smoking fish and can be used to add a unique twist to baked goods like pies and pastries.

Cherry Pellets:

Flavor Profile: Sweet, tart, mild.

Best Uses: Poultry, pork, beef, vegetables.

Description: Cherry pellets provide a slightly sweet and tart smoke that imparts a rich color and deep flavor to meats. This wood is versatile and works well with a variety of foods, adding a touch of sweetness that enhances both meats and vegetables. Cherry wood also gives a beautiful reddish hue to smoked meats, making them visually appealing.

Oak Pellets:

Flavor Profile: Medium, balanced, versatile.

Best Uses: Beef, pork, poultry, vegetables, bread.

Description: Oak pellets offer a balanced, moderate smoke that complements a wide range of foods. Its subtle smokiness is perfect for long smoking sessions, as it doesn't overpower the food. Oak is a great all-purpose wood that can be used with almost any type of meat and is particularly good for baking bread in the grill.

Blending Wood Pellets for Custom Flavors

One of the joys of using a Traeger grill is the ability to create custom pellet blends to suit your personal taste preferences. Here are a few suggested combinations and their ideal uses:

Hickory and Apple:

Flavor Profile: Robust smoke with a hint of sweetness.

Best Uses: Pork ribs, chicken, turkey.

Description: This blend combines the strong, smoky flavor of hickory with the sweet, fruity notes of apple. It's perfect for pork ribs, adding depth and sweetness to the rich, smoky flavor. It also works well with poultry, providing a balanced smoke that enhances the meat's natural flavors.

Cherry and Oak:

Flavor Profile: Sweet and balanced.

Best Uses: Beef, pork, vegetables.

Description: Cherry and oak create a well-rounded smoke flavor that is both sweet and robust. This combination is excellent for beef and pork, adding a touch of sweetness to the hearty, smoky flavor of oak. It's also great for smoking vegetables, providing a subtle yet complex flavor.

Mesquite and Apple:

Flavor Profile: Bold with a touch of sweetness.

Best Uses: Brisket, ribs, game meats.

Description: Mixing mesquite with apple moderates the intense earthiness of mesquite with the mild sweetness of apple. This blend is ideal for brisket and ribs, offering a bold smoke flavor with a sweet finish. It's also suitable for game meats, providing a complex, layered smoke.

Oak and Cherry:

Flavor Profile: Medium smoke with a hint of sweetness.

Best Uses: Poultry, beef, pork, bread.

Description: Oak's balanced smoke pairs well with cherry's mild sweetness, making this blend versatile and suitable for various foods. It's perfect for smoking poultry, beef, and pork, adding a nuanced flavor without overwhelming the meat. This blend is also great for baking bread, imparting a subtle, smoky aroma.

Maximizing Smoke Flavor

To get the most flavor from your wood pellets, it's important to understand a few key principles of smoking and grilling:

Temperature Control:

Maintaining a consistent temperature is crucial for optimal smoke absorption. Lower temperatures allow the smoke to penetrate the meat more deeply, enhancing its flavor. For most smoking recipes, aim for a temperature range of 225°F to 250°F.

Pre-Soaking Wood Pellets:

While not necessary with Traeger pellets, some grill masters prefer to soak their pellets in water for about 30 minutes before using them. This can help create more smoke, especially for short cooking times or when a more intense smoke flavor is desired.

Using a Water Pan:

Placing a pan of water in the grill helps maintain a stable cooking temperature and adds moisture to the cooking environment. This prevents the meat from drying out and enhances smoke absorption, resulting in juicier, more flavorful food.

Positioning the Food:

Arrange your food on the grill so it's exposed to the maximum amount of smoke. For larger cuts of meat, position them with the fattier side facing up. This allows the fat to render and baste the meat as it cooks, enhancing the flavor and tenderness.

Smoke Duration:

The duration of smoke exposure impacts the flavor intensity. While it's important not to over-smoke food (which can lead to a bitter taste), longer smoking times at lower temperatures generally produce a more pronounced smoke flavor. Use a combination of smoking and grilling techniques to achieve the desired taste.

Pairing Smoke with Spices and Marinades

Enhancing the flavor of your food with wood pellets is just one part of the equation. Pairing the right smoke with complementary spices, rubs, and marinades can elevate your dishes to new heights:

Spices and Rubs:

Create spice blends that complement the smoke flavor of your chosen pellets. For example, a rub with paprika, brown sugar, and chili powder pairs well with hickory smoke for pork ribs. For chicken, a blend of thyme, rosemary, and lemon zest enhances the mild sweetness of apple or cherry smoke.

Marinades:

Marinating your meat before smoking infuses it with additional flavors that work in harmony with the smoke. A citrus-based marinade with garlic and herbs pairs beautifully with mesquite smoke for beef. For poultry, try a marinade with soy sauce, ginger, and honey to complement the fruity smoke of apple pellets.

Glazes and Sauces:

Applying a glaze or sauce during the last stages of cooking adds a finishing touch that enhances the smoke flavor. For example, a honey-bourbon glaze works wonderfully with oak-smoked pork chops, while a tangy barbecue sauce complements the bold flavor of mesquite-smoked ribs.

Sustainability and Quality

Using high-quality, sustainable wood pellets is crucial for achieving the best flavor and ensuring your grill's longevity. Traeger's wood pellets are made from 100% natural hardwood, without any fillers or additives, providing a clean burn and pure smoke. Choosing sustainable pellets not only enhances your cooking experience but also supports responsible forest management practices.

By mastering the art of enhancing flavor with wood pellets and experimenting with different combinations and cooking techniques, you can unlock the full potential of your Traeger grill. Each type of wood pellet offers unique flavors that can be tailored to your personal preferences, allowing you to create delicious, memorable meals. Whether you're smoking a brisket, grilling a steak, or baking a pie, understanding the flavor profiles and best uses of each wood pellet will help you achieve the perfect taste every time.

Subchapter 6.1: Beef Recipes

Classic Smoked Brisket

Rub a 10-pound brisket with a blend of salt, pepper, garlic powder, and paprika. Preheat the Traeger to 225°F and smoke the brisket for 6 hours. Wrap in butcher paper and continue smoking for another 6-8 hours until the internal temperature reaches 203°F. Let it rest for 1 hour before slicing.

Perfect Ribeye Steaks

Season ribeye steaks with salt, pepper, and garlic powder. Preheat the Traeger to 450°F. Sear the steaks for 4-5 minutes per side until the internal temperature reaches 130°F for medium-rare. Let rest for 5 minutes before serving.

Beef Tenderloin Roast

Season a beef tenderloin with salt, pepper, and rosemary. Preheat the Traeger to 225°F and smoke the tenderloin for about 1.5 hours until the internal temperature reaches 130°F. Increase the heat to 450°F and sear for 5 minutes. Let rest before slicing.

Smoked Beef Short Ribs

Rub beef short ribs with a mix of salt, pepper, and garlic powder. Preheat the Traeger to 250°F. Smoke the ribs for 5-6 hours until the internal temperature reaches 205°F. Wrap in foil and rest for 30 minutes before serving.

Bacon-Wrapped Filet Mignon

Wrap each filet mignon with a slice of bacon and secure with a toothpick. Season with salt and pepper. Preheat the Traeger to 450°F. Sear the filets for 5-6 minutes per side until the internal temperature reaches 135°F for medium-rare. Let rest before serving.

Traeger Burgers

Season ground beef patties with salt, pepper, and garlic powder. Preheat the Traeger to 375°F. Grill the patties for 6-7 minutes per side until the internal temperature reaches 160°F. Serve on buns with your favorite toppings.

Beef Tri-Tip

Season a tri-tip roast with salt, pepper, and garlic powder. Preheat the Traeger to 225°F. Smoke the tri-tip for 2-3 hours until the internal temperature reaches 130°F. Increase the heat to 450°F and sear for 5 minutes. Let rest before slicing.

Smoked Meatloaf

Mix ground beef with breadcrumbs, egg, and your favorite seasonings. Shape into a loaf. Preheat the Traeger to 225°F. Smoke the meatloaf for 2-3 hours until the internal temperature reaches 160°F. Let rest for 10 minutes before slicing.

BBQ Beef Ribs

Rub beef ribs with a mix of salt, pepper, paprika, and brown sugar. Preheat the Traeger to 225°F. Smoke the ribs for 3 hours. Wrap in foil with a splash of apple juice and cook for another 2 hours. Unwrap and smoke for 1 more hour, basting with BBQ sauce.

Pepper-Crusted Prime Rib

Rub a prime rib roast with cracked black pepper, salt, and garlic powder. Preheat the Traeger to 250°F. Smoke the roast for 3-4 hours until the internal temperature reaches 125°F for medium-rare. Let rest for 30 minutes before slicing.

Smoked Beef Jerky

Marinate thin slices of beef in a mixture of soy sauce, brown sugar, garlic powder, and black pepper for 24 hours. Preheat the Traeger to 165°F. Smoke the beef strips for 4-5 hours until dry but still pliable.

Korean BBQ Beef Ribs

Marinate beef ribs in a mixture of soy sauce, brown sugar, sesame oil, garlic, and ginger for at least 4 hours. Preheat the Traeger to 375°F. Grill the ribs for 5-6 minutes per side until caramelized and cooked through.

Philly Cheesesteak

Slice ribeye thinly and season with salt and pepper. Preheat the Traeger to 400°F. Sauté onions and bell peppers, then cook the ribeye slices until done. Load into hoagie rolls, top with provolone cheese, and melt.

Beef Brisket Burnt Ends

Cut smoked brisket point into cubes. Toss with BBQ sauce and brown sugar. Preheat the Traeger to 275°F. Smoke the cubes for 2 hours until caramelized and tender. Serve as a delicious appetizer or main dish.

Teriyaki Beef Skewers

Marinate beef chunks in teriyaki sauce for at least 2 hours. Preheat the Traeger to 400°F. Thread the beef onto skewers and grill for 10-12 minutes, turning occasionally, until the beef is cooked to your liking. Serve with extra teriyaki sauce.

Pulled Pork

Rub a pork shoulder with a mix of salt, pepper, paprika, and garlic powder. Preheat the Traeger to 225°F. Smoke the pork shoulder for 12 hours or until it reaches an internal temperature of 195°F. Remove from the grill and let it rest for 30 minutes. Shred the pork with two forks, mixing in any remaining juices. Serve with your favorite BBQ sauce on buns or as a main dish.

Baby Back Ribs

Season baby back ribs with a blend of salt, pepper, paprika, and brown sugar. Preheat the Traeger to 225°F. Smoke the ribs for 3 hours. Wrap them in foil with a bit of apple juice and cook for another 2 hours. Unwrap and smoke for an additional hour, basting with BBQ sauce every 20 minutes. Serve hot.

Pork Tenderloin

Rub pork tenderloin with olive oil, salt, pepper, and rosemary. Preheat the Traeger to 225°F. Smoke the tenderloin for 2 hours or until the internal temperature reaches 145°F. Increase the heat to 450°F and sear the tenderloin for 5 minutes to develop a crust. Let it rest for 10 minutes before slicing and serving.

Smoked Ham

Score the surface of the ham and apply a glaze made of honey, brown sugar, and mustard. Preheat the Traeger to 250°F. Smoke the ham for 3-4 hours until the internal temperature reaches 140°F. Baste with additional glaze every hour. Let the ham rest for 15 minutes before slicing and serving.

Pork Belly Burnt Ends

Cut pork belly into 1-inch cubes. Toss with salt, pepper, and your favorite BBQ rub. Preheat the Traeger to 275°F. Smoke the pork belly cubes for 3 hours. Toss the cubes in BBQ sauce and brown sugar, then return to the grill for another hour. Serve as a delicious appetizer or main dish.

Stuffed Pork Chops

Cut a pocket into each pork chop and stuff with a mixture of spinach, cream cheese, and garlic. Season the outside with salt and pepper. Preheat the Traeger to 350°F. Smoke the pork chops for 45 minutes to 1 hour until the internal temperature reaches 145°F. Let them rest for a few minutes before serving.

Smoked Pork Shoulder

Rub a pork shoulder with a blend of salt, pepper, paprika, and garlic powder. Preheat the Traeger to 225°F. Smoke the pork shoulder for 12-14 hours until it reaches an internal temperature of 195°F. Let it rest for 30 minutes, then shred the meat. Serve with BBQ sauce on buns or as a main dish.

Bacon-Wrapped Pork Loin

Wrap a pork loin with bacon and secure with toothpicks. Season with salt, pepper, and garlic powder. Preheat the Traeger to 325°F. Smoke the pork loin for 2-3 hours until the internal temperature reaches 145°F. Let it rest for 10 minutes before slicing and serving.

Honey-Glazed Ham

Score the surface of the ham and brush with a honey and mustard glaze. Preheat the Traeger to 250°F. Smoke the ham for 3-4 hours until the internal temperature reaches 140°F. Baste with additional glaze every hour. Let the ham rest for 15 minutes before slicing and serving.

Smoked Sausage

Place sausages directly on the grill grates. Preheat the Traeger to 225°F. Smoke the sausages for 1.5-2 hours until the internal temperature reaches 160°F. Serve hot with mustard and sauerkraut.

BBQ Pork Ribs

Season pork ribs with a blend of salt, pepper, paprika, and brown sugar. Preheat the Traeger to 225°F. Smoke the ribs for 3 hours. Wrap them in foil with apple juice and cook for another 2 hours. Unwrap and smoke for an additional hour, basting with BBQ sauce every 20 minutes. Serve hot.

Pork Carnitas

Season pork shoulder with salt, pepper, cumin, and oregano. Preheat the Traeger to 275°F. Smoke the pork shoulder for 4-5 hours until the internal temperature reaches 195°F. Shred the meat and crisp it up in a hot skillet. Serve in tortillas with your favorite toppings.

Maple Bacon

Brush thick-cut bacon slices with maple syrup. Preheat the Traeger to 225°F. Smoke the bacon for 1.5-2 hours until crispy. Let cool slightly before serving.

Smoked Pork Belly

Rub pork belly with salt, pepper, and paprika. Preheat the Traeger to 225°F. Smoke the pork belly for 4 hours until tender. Increase the heat to 450°F and sear for 5-10 minutes to develop a crispy crust. Let rest before slicing and serving.

Sweet and Spicy Pork Chops

Rub pork chops with a mixture of brown sugar, chili powder, and garlic powder. Preheat the Traeger to 350°F. Smoke the pork chops for 45 minutes to 1 hour until the internal temperature reaches 145°F. Let them rest for a few minutes before serving.

Whole Smoked Chicken

Rub a whole chicken with olive oil, salt, pepper, and garlic powder. Preheat the Traeger to 225°F. Smoke the chicken for 3-4 hours until the internal temperature in the breast reaches 165°F. Baste with melted butter during the last hour for extra flavor. Let it rest for 15 minutes before carving and serving.

Chicken Wings

Toss chicken wings with a mixture of salt, pepper, paprika, and garlic powder. Preheat the Traeger to 350°F. Smoke the wings for 1.5-2 hours until crispy and cooked through. Toss in your favorite BBQ or buffalo sauce before serving.

Smoked Turkey Breast

Rub a turkey breast with olive oil, salt, pepper, and rosemary. Preheat the Traeger to 225°F. Smoke the turkey breast for 3-4 hours until the internal temperature reaches 165°F. Let it rest for 15 minutes before slicing and serving.

Spatchcocked Turkey

Remove the backbone from a turkey and flatten it. Rub with olive oil, salt, pepper, and garlic powder. Preheat the Traeger to 225°F. Smoke the turkey for 4-5 hours until the internal temperature reaches 165°F. Let it rest for 20 minutes before carving.

Chicken Thighs

Season chicken thighs with salt, pepper, and paprika. Preheat the Traeger to 350°F. Smoke the thighs for 1.5-2 hours until the internal temperature reaches 165°F. Baste with BBQ sauce during the last 30 minutes for extra flavor.

Duck Breast

Score the skin of duck breasts and season with salt and pepper. Preheat the Traeger to 225°F. Smoke the duck breasts for 1.5-2 hours until the internal temperature reaches 135°F for medium-rare. Let rest for 10 minutes before slicing.

Beer Can Chicken

Season a whole chicken with salt, pepper, and garlic powder. Insert an open can of beer into the cavity. Preheat the Traeger to 375°F. Smoke the chicken upright for 1.5-2 hours until the internal temperature reaches 165°F. Let rest before carving.

Chicken Kabobs

Thread chicken pieces, bell peppers, and onions onto skewers. Season with salt, pepper, and paprika. Preheat the Traeger to 350°F. Smoke the kabobs for 20-25 minutes until the chicken is cooked through and the vegetables are tender.

BBQ Chicken Drumsticks

Season chicken drumsticks with salt, pepper, and paprika. Preheat the Traeger to 350°F. Smoke the drumsticks for 1.5 hours until the internal temperature reaches 165°F. Baste with BBQ sauce during the last 30 minutes for extra flavor.

Cedar Plank Chicken

Soak a cedar plank in water for 1 hour. Season chicken breasts with salt, pepper, and lemon zest. Preheat the Traeger to 350°F. Place the chicken on the cedar plank and smoke for 45-60 minutes until the internal temperature reaches 165°F.

Smoked Chicken Breast

Rub chicken breasts with olive oil, salt, pepper, and paprika. Preheat the Traeger to 225°F. Smoke the chicken breasts for 1.5-2 hours until the internal temperature reaches 165°F. Let rest for 10 minutes before slicing and serving.

Grilled Quail

Marinate quail in olive oil, lemon juice, garlic, and rosemary for 2 hours. Preheat the Traeger to 400°F. Grill the quail for 15-20 minutes until the internal temperature reaches 165°F, turning occasionally for even cooking.

Stuffed Turkey Breast

Butterfly a turkey breast and stuff with a mixture of spinach, feta, and garlic. Roll and tie with kitchen twine. Season with salt and pepper. Preheat the Traeger to 350°F. Smoke the stuffed breast for 1.5-2 hours until the internal temperature reaches 165°F. Let rest before slicing.

Smoked Chicken Tacos

Rub chicken breasts with chili powder, cumin, and garlic powder. Preheat the Traeger to 225°F. Smoke the chicken for 1.5-2 hours until the internal temperature reaches 165°F. Shred the chicken and serve in tortillas with your favorite taco toppings.

Herb-Roasted Chicken

Rub a whole chicken with olive oil, salt, pepper, and a mix of rosemary, thyme, and sage. Preheat the Traeger to 350°F. Smoke the chicken for 1.5-2 hours until the internal temperature reaches 165°F. Let rest for 15 minutes before carving and serving.

Subchapter 6.4: Seafood Recipes

Cedar Plank Salmon

Soak a cedar plank in water for 1 hour. Season salmon fillets with olive oil, salt, pepper, and lemon zest. Preheat the Traeger to 350°F. Place the salmon on the cedar plank and smoke for 25-30 minutes until the internal temperature reaches 145°F. Garnish with fresh dill and lemon slices before serving.

Smoked Shrimp

Toss shrimp with olive oil, garlic, salt, and pepper. Preheat the Traeger to 225°F. Arrange the shrimp on a baking sheet and smoke for 30-45 minutes until pink and firm. Serve with cocktail sauce or melted butter.

Grilled Lobster Tails

Split lobster tails and brush with garlic butter. Preheat the Traeger to 375°F. Grill the lobster tails shell side down for 20-25 minutes until the meat is opaque and reaches an internal temperature of 145°F. Baste with more garlic butter during cooking.

Smoked Trout

Season trout fillets with salt, pepper, and lemon zest. Preheat the Traeger to 180°F. Smoke the trout for 1.5-2 hours until the internal temperature reaches 145°F. Serve with lemon wedges and fresh dill.

Grilled Scallops

Pat scallops dry and season with salt, pepper, and olive oil. Preheat the Traeger to 400°F. Grill the scallops for 2-3 minutes per side until opaque and slightly firm. Serve with a squeeze of lemon juice.

Smoked Crab Legs

Brush crab legs with melted butter and sprinkle with Old Bay seasoning. Preheat the Traeger to 225°F. Smoke the crab legs for 25-30 minutes until heated through. Serve with additional melted butter for dipping.

Grilled Oysters

Shuck oysters and place them on a baking sheet. Top each oyster with a pat of garlic butter and a sprinkle of Parmesan cheese. Preheat the Traeger to 450°F. Grill the oysters for 5-7 minutes until the cheese is melted and bubbly.

Fish Tacos

Season white fish fillets with chili powder, cumin, and salt. Preheat the Traeger to 375°F. Grill the fish for 10-12 minutes until cooked through and flaky. Serve in tortillas with cabbage slaw, avocado, and lime wedges.

Smoked Swordfish

Season swordfish steaks with olive oil, salt, and pepper. Preheat the Traeger to 225°F. Smoke the swordfish for 1 hour until the internal temperature reaches 145°F. Serve with a drizzle of lemon butter sauce.

BBQ Salmon Burgers

Mix ground salmon with breadcrumbs, egg, green onions, and dill. Form into patties. Preheat the Traeger to 375°F. Grill the patties for 5-7 minutes per side until cooked through. Serve on buns with lettuce, tomato, and tartar sauce.

Grilled Clams

Clean clams and place them in a foil packet with garlic, butter, and white wine. Preheat the Traeger to 400°F. Grill the clams for 10-15 minutes until they open. Discard any that do not open and serve with the cooking liquid.

Smoked Mahi Mahi

Season mahi mahi fillets with olive oil, salt, and pepper. Preheat the Traeger to 225°F. Smoke the fillets for 1.5 hours until the internal temperature reaches 145°F. Serve with a fresh mango salsa.

Grilled Tuna Steaks

Brush tuna steaks with olive oil and season with salt and pepper. Preheat the Traeger to 450°F. Grill the tuna for 2-3 minutes per side for medium-rare. Serve with a soy-ginger sauce.

Smoked Octopus

Boil octopus in water with lemon and bay leaves for 40 minutes. Preheat the Traeger to 225°F. Smoke the octopus for 1 hour. Finish by grilling at 450°F for 5 minutes per side. Serve with a drizzle of olive oil and lemon.

Garlic Butter Shrimp

Toss shrimp with melted garlic butter, salt, and pepper. Preheat the Traeger to 350°F. Grill the shrimp for 5-7 minutes until pink and firm. Serve with additional garlic butter for dipping.

Subchapter 6.5: Vegetarian Recipes

Grilled Portobello Mushrooms

Brush portobello mushrooms with olive oil and season with salt, pepper, and garlic powder. Preheat the Traeger to 375°F. Grill the mushrooms for 10-12 minutes, turning once, until tender and slightly charred. Serve as a side dish or burger substitute.

Smoked Stuffed Peppers

Stuff bell peppers with a mixture of rice, black beans, corn, and cheese. Preheat the Traeger to 250°F. Smoke the peppers for 1.5-2 hours until the peppers are tender and the filling is heated through. Garnish with cilantro and serve.

Grilled Corn on the Cob

Husk the corn and brush with melted butter. Preheat the Traeger to 375°F. Grill the corn for 20-25 minutes, turning occasionally, until tender and slightly charred. Brush with more butter and sprinkle with salt before serving.

Smoked Mac and Cheese

Prepare mac and cheese in a cast iron skillet. Top with breadcrumbs and extra cheese. Preheat the Traeger to 225°F. Smoke the mac and cheese for 1 hour until bubbly and golden brown. Let cool slightly before serving.

Grilled Asparagus

Toss asparagus spears with olive oil, salt, and pepper. Preheat the Traeger to 400°F. Grill the asparagus for 10-12 minutes, turning occasionally, until tender and slightly charred. Serve hot with a squeeze of lemon juice.

Smoked Eggplant Parmesan

Slice eggplant and brush with olive oil. Preheat the Traeger to 225°F. Smoke the eggplant slices for 1 hour. Layer in a baking dish with marinara sauce and mozzarella cheese. Bake at 350°F for 30 minutes until bubbly.

Veggie Skewers

Thread cherry tomatoes, bell peppers, zucchini, and mushrooms onto skewers. Brush with olive oil and season with salt and pepper. Preheat the Traeger to 375°F. Grill the skewers for 15-20 minutes, turning occasionally, until vegetables are tender.

Grilled Cauliflower Steaks

Slice cauliflower into 1-inch steaks. Brush with olive oil and season with salt, pepper, and paprika. Preheat the Traeger to 375°F. Grill the cauliflower for 20-25 minutes, turning once, until tender and slightly charred.

BBQ Tofu

Press tofu to remove excess moisture and cut into cubes. Toss with BBQ sauce. Preheat the Traeger to 375°F. Grill the tofu for 20-25 minutes, turning occasionally, until crispy and caramelized. Serve with extra BBQ sauce.

Smoked Sweet Potatoes

Rub sweet potatoes with olive oil and pierce with a fork. Preheat the Traeger to 225°F. Smoke the sweet potatoes for 2 hours until tender. Serve with butter, cinnamon, and brown sugar.

Grilled Zucchini

Slice zucchini lengthwise and brush with olive oil. Season with salt, pepper, and garlic powder. Preheat the Traeger to 375°F. Grill the zucchini for 10-12 minutes, turning once, until tender and slightly charred.

Smoked Brussels Sprouts

Toss halved Brussels sprouts with olive oil, salt, and pepper. Preheat the Traeger to 225°F. Smoke the Brussels sprouts for 1 hour until tender. Increase heat to 400°F and grill for an additional 10 minutes to caramelize.

Grilled Avocado

Cut avocados in half and remove the pit. Brush with olive oil and season with salt and pepper. Preheat the Traeger to 375°F. Grill the avocados for 5-7 minutes, cut side down, until grill marks appear. Serve with lime juice.

Stuffed Acorn Squash

Cut acorn squash in half and remove seeds. Stuff with a mixture of quinoa, cranberries, and pecans. Preheat the Traeger to 375°F. Smoke the squash for 1.5-2 hours until tender. Drizzle with maple syrup before serving.

Smoked Ratatouille

Slice zucchini, eggplant, and tomatoes. Layer in a cast iron skillet with olive oil, garlic, and herbs. Preheat the Traeger to 225°F. Smoke the vegetables for 2 hours until tender. Serve as a side dish or main course.

Subchapter 6.6: Appetizers and Sides

Jalapeño Poppers

Halve jalapeños and remove seeds. Stuff with a mixture of cream cheese and shredded cheddar. Wrap each with a slice of bacon and secure with a toothpick. Preheat the Traeger to 350°F. Grill the poppers for 20-25 minutes until bacon is crispy.

Smoked Queso Dip

In a cast iron skillet, combine Velveeta, shredded cheddar, diced tomatoes with green chilies, and cooked sausage. Preheat the Traeger to 225°F. Smoke the dip for 1 hour until melted and bubbly. Stir occasionally and serve with tortilla chips.

Grilled Bruschetta

Brush slices of baguette with olive oil and grill at 400°F for 2-3 minutes per side. Top with diced tomatoes, garlic, basil, and balsamic glaze. Serve immediately as a delicious appetizer.

Smoked Deviled Eggs

Hard boil eggs and cool. Halve and remove yolks. Mix yolks with mayo, mustard, and smoked paprika. Refill egg whites with yolk mixture. Preheat the Traeger to 180°F. Smoke the filled eggs for 30 minutes. Chill before serving.

BBQ Baked Beans

In a cast iron skillet, combine canned baked beans, BBQ sauce, brown sugar, and diced bacon. Preheat the Traeger to 225°F. Smoke the beans for 2 hours, stirring occasionally. Serve hot as a classic BBQ side.

Grilled Artichokes

Halve and steam artichokes until tender. Brush with olive oil and season with salt, pepper, and garlic powder. Preheat the Traeger to 400°F. Grill the artichokes for 5-7 minutes per side. Serve with lemon aioli.

Smoked Potato Salad

Boil baby potatoes until tender. Toss with olive oil, salt, and pepper. Preheat the Traeger to 225°F. Smoke the potatoes for 1 hour. Mix with mayo, mustard, celery, and green onions. Chill before serving.

Cornbread

Mix cornbread batter according to package instructions. Pour into a cast iron skillet. Preheat the Traeger to 375°F. Bake the cornbread for 25-30 minutes until golden brown and a toothpick inserted comes out clean. Serve warm.

BBQ Nachos

Layer tortilla chips with shredded cheese, pulled pork, jalapeños, and BBQ sauce. Preheat the Traeger to 350°F. Grill the nachos for 10-15 minutes until cheese is melted. Top with sour cream and green onions.

Grilled Flatbread

Brush flatbread with olive oil and top with garlic, tomatoes, and mozzarella. Preheat the Traeger to 375°F. Grill the flatbread for 10-12 minutes until the cheese is melted and bubbly. Garnish with fresh basil.

Smoked Salsa

Combine diced tomatoes, onions, jalapeños, and garlic. Preheat the Traeger to 225°F. Smoke the mixture for 1 hour. Blend with cilantro, lime juice, and salt. Chill before serving with tortilla chips.

Grilled Stuffed Mushrooms

Remove stems from mushrooms and stuff with a mixture of cream cheese, garlic, and breadcrumbs. Preheat the Traeger to 350°F. Grill the mushrooms for 20 minutes until the filling is hot and bubbly.

Smoked Guacamole

Mash avocados with lime juice, salt, and pepper. Stir in diced smoked tomatoes and onions. Preheat the Traeger to 225°F. Smoke the guacamole for 30 minutes. Serve with tortilla chips.

BBQ Corn Fritters

Mix corn kernels, flour, eggs, and green onions into a batter. Preheat the Traeger to 375°F. Drop spoonfuls of batter onto a griddle and cook for 2-3 minutes per side until golden brown. Serve with BBQ sauce.

Grilled Pita and Hummus

Brush pita bread with olive oil and grill at 375°F for 2-3 minutes per side until warm and slightly charred. Serve with homemade or store-bought hummus.

Subchapter 6.7: Desserts

Smoked Apple Pie

Prepare apple pie filling with sliced apples, sugar, cinnamon, and nutmeg. Pour into a pie crust. Preheat the Traeger to 350°F. Smoke the pie for 1.5-2 hours until the crust is golden brown and the filling is bubbly. Let cool before serving.

Grilled Peaches

Halve and pit peaches. Brush with melted butter and sprinkle with brown sugar. Preheat the Traeger to 375°F. Grill the peaches for 10-15 minutes until tender and caramelized. Serve with vanilla ice cream.

Smoked Cheesecake

Prepare a cheesecake filling and pour into a graham cracker crust. Preheat the Traeger to 225°F. Smoke the cheesecake for 1.5-2 hours until set. Let cool and refrigerate for at least 4 hours before serving.

Grilled Pineapple

Cut pineapple into rings and brush with brown sugar and cinnamon. Preheat the Traeger to 375°F. Grill the pineapple for 5-7 minutes per side until caramelized. Serve warm with a scoop of ice cream.

Smoked Chocolate Cake

Prepare chocolate cake batter and pour into a greased cake pan. Preheat the Traeger to 350°F. Smoke the cake for 1 hour until a toothpick inserted comes out clean. Let cool before frosting and serving.

BBQ S'mores

Layer graham crackers, chocolate, and marshmallows on a baking sheet. Preheat the Traeger to 350°F. Grill for 5-7 minutes until the marshmallows are melted and golden brown. Serve warm.

Smoked Bread Pudding

Cube bread and mix with eggs, milk, sugar, and cinnamon. Pour into a baking dish. Preheat the Traeger to 350°F. Smoke the bread pudding for 1 hour until set. Serve warm with caramel sauce.

Grilled Banana Split

Halve bananas lengthwise and grill at 375°F for 3-4 minutes per side. Place grilled bananas in a bowl and top with ice cream, chocolate syrup, whipped cream, and cherries.

Smoked Brownies

Prepare brownie batter and pour into a greased pan. Preheat the Traeger to 325°F. Smoke the brownies for 30-35 minutes until a toothpick inserted comes out clean. Let cool before cutting into squares.

Grilled Mango

Slice mango into thick strips and brush with honey. Preheat the Traeger to 375°F. Grill the mango for 4-5 minutes per side until caramelized. Serve with a sprinkle of chili powder.

Smoked Pecan Pie

Prepare pecan pie filling and pour into a pie crust. Preheat the Traeger to 350°F. Smoke the pie for 1.5 hours until the filling is set and the crust is golden. Let cool before serving.

Grilled Watermelon

Cut watermelon into thick slices and brush with olive oil. Preheat the Traeger to 375°F. Grill the watermelon for 2-3 minutes per side until grill marks appear. Serve with a sprinkle of salt.

Smoked Lemon Bars

Prepare lemon bar filling and pour over a shortbread crust. Preheat the Traeger to 325°F. Smoke the lemon bars for 35-40 minutes until set. Let cool and dust with powdered sugar before cutting.

Grilled Cinnamon Apples

Core and slice apples. Toss with melted butter, cinnamon, and sugar. Preheat the Traeger to 375°F. Grill the apples for 10-15 minutes until tender and caramelized. Serve warm with whipped cream.

Smoked Pears

Halve and core pears. Brush with honey and sprinkle with cinnamon. Preheat the Traeger to 225°F. Smoke the pears for 1 hour until tender. Serve with a dollop of mascarpone cheese.

Classic BBQ Sauce

Combine 2 cups ketchup, 1/2 cup apple cider vinegar, 1/2 cup brown sugar, 1/4 cup honey, 1 tablespoon Worcestershire sauce, 1 tablespoon lemon juice, 1 teaspoon smoked paprika, and 1 teaspoon garlic powder. Simmer over medium heat for 20 minutes until thickened. Cool and store in a jar.

Spicy Texas Rub

Mix 1/4 cup brown sugar, 1/4 cup paprika, 2 tablespoons black pepper, 2 tablespoons salt, 1 tablespoon chili powder, 1 tablespoon garlic powder, 1 tablespoon onion powder, and 1 teaspoon cayenne pepper. Store in an airtight container.

Carolina Mustard Sauce

Combine 1 cup yellow mustard, 1/2 cup apple cider vinegar, 1/4 cup honey, 1/4 cup brown sugar, 1 tablespoon Worcestershire sauce, 1 teaspoon garlic powder, 1 teaspoon onion powder, and 1/2 teaspoon cayenne pepper. Simmer over medium heat for 10 minutes. Cool and store in a jar.

Kansas City BBQ Sauce

Combine 2 cups ketchup, 1/2 cup molasses, 1/2 cup brown sugar, 1/2 cup apple cider vinegar, 1 tablespoon Worcestershire sauce, 1 tablespoon liquid smoke, 1 teaspoon garlic powder, 1 teaspoon onion powder, and 1/2 teaspoon black pepper. Simmer for 20 minutes. Cool and store in a jar.

Memphis Dry Rub

Mix 1/4 cup paprika, 2 tablespoons brown sugar, 2 tablespoons black pepper, 1 tablespoon salt, 1 tablespoon chili powder, 1 tablespoon garlic powder, 1 tablespoon onion powder, and 1 teaspoon cayenne pepper. Store in an airtight container.

Honey Garlic Glaze

Combine 1/2 cup honey, 1/4 cup soy sauce, 1 tablespoon minced garlic, 1 tablespoon apple cider vinegar, and 1 teaspoon grated ginger. Simmer for 10 minutes until slightly thickened. Cool and store in a jar.

Smoky Chipotle Sauce

Blend 1 cup mayonnaise, 2 chipotle peppers in adobo sauce, 2 tablespoons lime juice, 1 tablespoon honey, and 1 teaspoon smoked paprika until smooth. Store in an airtight container.

Herb Butter Rub

Mix 1/2 cup softened butter with 2 tablespoons chopped parsley, 1 tablespoon chopped thyme, 1 tablespoon chopped rosemary, 1 teaspoon garlic powder, 1 teaspoon lemon zest, and 1/2 teaspoon salt. Use immediately or store in the refrigerator.

Sweet and Spicy BBQ Sauce

Combine 2 cups ketchup, 1/2 cup honey, 1/4 cup apple cider vinegar, 1/4 cup brown sugar, 1 tablespoon Worcestershire sauce, 1 tablespoon hot sauce, 1 teaspoon garlic powder, and 1/2 teaspoon cayenne pepper. Simmer for 20 minutes. Cool and store in a jar.

Apple Cider Vinegar Sauce

Combine 1 cup apple cider vinegar, 1/4 cup ketchup, 1/4 cup brown sugar, 1 tablespoon hot sauce, 1 teaspoon red pepper flakes, 1 teaspoon black pepper, and 1 teaspoon salt. Mix well and store in a jar.

Cajun Rub

Mix 2 tablespoons paprika, 1 tablespoon salt, 1 tablespoon garlic powder, 1 tablespoon onion powder, 1 tablespoon black pepper, 1 tablespoon cayenne pepper, 1 tablespoon dried oregano, and 1 tablespoon dried thyme. Store in an airtight container.

Asian Teriyaki Sauce

Combine 1/2 cup soy sauce, 1/4 cup brown sugar, 1/4 cup mirin, 1 tablespoon grated ginger, 1 tablespoon minced garlic, and 1 teaspoon sesame oil. Simmer for 10 minutes until slightly thickened. Cool and store in a jar.

Chapter 7: Advanced Grilling Techniques

Smoking Techniques

Mastering advanced grilling techniques opens up a new world of flavors and textures in your culinary repertoire. Among these, smoking techniques are essential for achieving deep, rich flavors in your grilled foods. Smoking can be categorized into two main types: cold smoking and hot smoking.

Cold smoking involves smoking foods at temperatures below 90°F for extended periods, infusing them with a smoky flavor without cooking them. This technique is ideal for items like cheese, nuts, and cured meats. Cold smoking requires a smoke generator that can produce smoke without raising the temperature significantly.

Hot smoking, on the other hand, cooks and smokes the food simultaneously at temperatures between 225°F and 275°F. This method is perfect for meats such as brisket, ribs, and poultry. Hot smoking not only adds a smoky flavor but also tenderizes the meat, making it juicy and flavorful.

Different types of meat require specific smoking techniques. For instance, a brisket benefits from a low and slow approach, smoking at 225°F for 10-14 hours until it reaches an internal temperature of 203°F. Pork ribs, meanwhile, can be smoked at 225°F for about 6 hours using the 3-2-1 method: 3 hours of smoking, 2 hours wrapped in foil, and 1 hour with sauce. Poultry, like chicken or turkey, can be smoked at slightly higher temperatures around 250°F to ensure the skin gets crispy while the meat remains tender and juicy.

By understanding and mastering these smoking techniques, you can elevate your grilling game, creating dishes that are not only flavorful but also cooked to perfection.

Using Accessories

Using accessories can significantly enhance your grilling experience and help you achieve professional-level results. Grill accessories like grill mats, smoker tubes, and other tools offer versatility and convenience, making it easier to experiment with different cooking techniques and recipes.

Grill mats are non-stick surfaces that can be placed directly on the grill grates. They are perfect for cooking delicate foods such as fish, vegetables, and small items that might fall through the grates. Grill mats also make cleanup easier, as they prevent food from sticking and keep the grill grates cleaner.

Smoker tubes are cylindrical metal tubes filled with wood pellets. When placed on the grill, they generate smoke for several hours, adding a smoky flavor to your food without the need for a dedicated smoker. Smoker tubes are ideal for cold smoking and enhancing the smoke flavor in hot smoking applications.

Other useful accessories include meat probes, grill thermometers, and rotisserie kits. Meat probes and grill thermometers help you monitor the internal temperature of your food and the grill, ensuring precise cooking. Rotisserie kits allow you to cook whole chickens, roasts, and other large cuts of meat evenly, resulting in juicy, flavorful dishes.

Using these accessories can take your grilling to the next level by providing more control and expanding your cooking options. Whether you're smoking, grilling, or roasting, the right tools can help you achieve consistent, delicious results every time. Investing in quality accessories and learning how to use them effectively will enhance your overall grilling experience and allow you to explore a wide range of culinary possibilities.

Chapter 8: Maintenance and Care

Cleaning Your Traeger Grill

Proper maintenance and care are essential for keeping your Traeger grill in top condition and ensuring it delivers optimal performance over the long term. Regular cleaning not only prolongs the life of your grill but also enhances the flavor of your food by preventing the buildup of grease and ash. Here's a step-by-step cleaning guide and some tips to help you maintain your Traeger grill.

Step-by-Step Cleaning Guide:

1. **Cool Down**: Before starting any cleaning, ensure the grill is completely cool to avoid burns and accidents.

2. **Empty the Hopper**: Remove any unused pellets from the hopper. This prevents them from absorbing moisture and degrading in quality.

3. **Clean the Grill Grates**: Remove the grates and scrape off any food residue using a grill brush. Soak them in warm, soapy water for a deeper clean, then rinse and dry thoroughly.

4. **Clean the Drip Tray and Heat Baffle**: Remove the drip tray and heat baffle. Scrape off any grease buildup using a plastic scraper. If they are heavily soiled, soak them in warm, soapy water, then rinse and dry.

5. **Vacuum the Firepot**: Use a shop vacuum to remove ash and debris from the firepot. Regularly cleaning the firepot ensures proper airflow and ignition.

6. **Wipe Down the Interior**: Wipe down the interior walls of the grill with a damp cloth. Avoid using harsh chemicals, as they can damage the grill's surface and affect the taste of your food.

7. **Clean the Exterior**: Use a mild detergent and water to clean the exterior of the grill. Dry thoroughly to prevent rust.

8. **Check the Grease Management System**: Ensure the grease management system, including the drip bucket, is clean and free of obstructions. Replace the foil lining the drip tray regularly to make cleaning easier.

Tips for Prolonging the Life of Your Grill:

1. **Regular Cleaning**: Clean your grill after every few uses to prevent the buildup of grease and ash, which can affect performance and flavor.

2. **Protect from the Elements**: Use a grill cover to protect your Traeger from rain, snow, and UV rays. This prevents rust and prolongs the life of the grill.

3. **Inspect and Replace Parts**: Regularly inspect components like the gaskets, heat baffle, and firepot for wear and tear. Replace any damaged parts promptly to ensure optimal performance.

4. **Store Pellets Properly**: Keep wood pellets in a dry, airtight container to prevent moisture absorption, which can cause poor combustion and inconsistent temperatures.

5. **Perform Regular Maintenance**: Periodically check the wiring and connections, especially around the controller and auger. Ensure there are no loose connections or signs of wear.

By following this step-by-step cleaning guide and incorporating these maintenance tips, you can ensure your Traeger grill remains in excellent condition, delivering delicious, smoky flavors for years to come. Regular care not only enhances the longevity of your grill but also ensures that every meal you cook is safe and tastes its best.

Routine Maintenance

Regular maintenance of your Traeger grill is crucial to ensure it operates efficiently and delivers consistently delicious results. Routine checks and maintenance tasks help prevent common issues and extend the lifespan of your grill. Here's a comprehensive guide to routine maintenance and troubleshooting common problems.

Regular Checks and Maintenance Tasks:

1. **Check Pellet Quality**: Always use high-quality Traeger pellets. Poor-quality pellets can produce excess ash and inconsistent temperatures. Store pellets in a dry, airtight container to prevent moisture absorption.

2. **Inspect the Firepot**: After every few uses, inspect the firepot for ash buildup. A clogged firepot can impede airflow and cause ignition problems. Use a shop vacuum to remove ash and debris.

3. **Clean the Grease Management System**: Regularly check the drip tray and grease bucket. Empty and clean the bucket and replace the aluminum

foil on the drip tray to prevent grease fires and ensure efficient grease management.

4. **Examine the Auger and Hopper**: Ensure the auger is feeding pellets smoothly. Occasionally empty the hopper to check for pellet jams or debris. Clean the auger tube if pellets are not feeding correctly.

5. **Monitor the Temperature Probe**: Wipe down the temperature probe inside the grill with a damp cloth to remove grease and residue. A dirty probe can give inaccurate temperature readings.

6. **Check the Gaskets and Seals**: Inspect the gaskets around the lid and hopper. Replace any worn or damaged gaskets to maintain proper heat and smoke retention.

7. **Clean the Grill Grates**: After each use, scrape the grates clean. Periodically, give them a deep clean by soaking them in warm, soapy water, then rinsing and drying thoroughly.

Troubleshooting Common Issues:

1. **Temperature Fluctuations**: If your grill experiences temperature swings, check for pellet quality and ensure the firepot is clean. Wind and weather conditions can also affect temperature; consider using a grill blanket in cold weather.

2. **Ignition Problems**: If the grill fails to ignite, inspect the firepot for ash buildup and ensure the hot rod is functioning. If the hot rod is damaged, replace it. Verify that the auger is feeding pellets correctly.

3. **Uneven Cooking**: Uneven heat distribution can result from blocked airflow. Ensure the heat baffle and drip tray are properly positioned and free of obstructions. Clean the grill grates and interior walls to improve airflow.

4. **Pellet Jams**: If pellets aren't feeding smoothly, empty the hopper and inspect the auger tube for jams. Clear any blockages and ensure the pellets are dry and of good quality. Occasionally, run the auger in reverse to dislodge any stuck pellets.

5. **Smoke Issues**: If the grill is producing too much or too little smoke, check the pellet quality and cleanliness of the firepot. Adjust the P-setting on the controller to regulate pellet feed rate and smoke output.

By performing these regular checks and maintenance tasks, you can prevent common issues and keep your Traeger grill in top working condition. Troubleshooting minor problems as they arise will ensure consistent performance and prolong the life of your grill, allowing you to enjoy perfectly smoked and grilled foods for years to come.

Chapter 9: Sourcing and Preparing Ingredients

Choosing quality meat is the cornerstone of exceptional grilling and smoking. The right cuts, properly selected and prepared, can make a significant difference in the taste and tenderness of your dishes. Understanding how to select the best cuts of meat and interpret meat grades and labels will ensure you consistently achieve outstanding results with your Traeger grill.

Choosing Quality Meat:

When selecting meat, several factors should be considered to ensure you get the best quality. Look for meat that is fresh, with a bright color and minimal liquid in the packaging. The meat should feel firm to the touch and have a clean, slightly sweet smell. Avoid any meat that looks grayish, has a strong odor, or feels slimy.

How to Select the Best Cuts of Meat:

Different cuts of meat offer varying textures and flavors, and knowing which cuts are best for grilling or smoking can enhance your cooking.

1. **Beef**:

    - **Brisket**: Ideal for smoking due to its high fat content and connective tissue, which break down and become tender over long, slow cooking.

    - **Ribeye**: A favorite for grilling because of its marbling, which ensures a juicy, flavorful steak.

    - **Tenderloin (Filet Mignon)**: Known for its tenderness, it's best grilled quickly to avoid drying out.

2. **Pork**:

- Shoulder (Boston Butt): Perfect for pulled pork, this cut benefits from long, slow cooking that breaks down its marbling and connective tissue.

- Ribs: Baby back ribs and spare ribs are excellent for smoking, offering a balance of meat and fat that results in tender, flavorful bites.

- Loin: This lean cut is great for quick grilling or roasting, but it should be cooked carefully to avoid drying out.

3. Poultry:

- Whole Chicken: Smoking a whole chicken provides a balance of dark and white meat, all infused with smoky flavor.

- Thighs: These dark meat pieces are flavorful and stay moist during smoking or grilling.

- Breasts: Lean and versatile, best brined or marinated before grilling to ensure they remain juicy.

Understanding Meat Grades and Labels:

Meat grading and labeling provide insight into the quality and characteristics of the meat, helping you make informed choices.

1. Beef Grades:

- Prime: The highest grade, with abundant marbling, making it the best choice for grilling and roasting.

- Choice: Less marbling than Prime but still high quality, suitable for most cooking methods.

- **Select**: Leaner than Choice, often requires careful cooking to avoid dryness.

2. **Pork Labels**:

    - **Certified Organic**: Raised without antibiotics or synthetic hormones, fed organic feed.

    - **Natural**: Minimally processed without artificial ingredients.

    - **Heritage**: From traditional breeds known for their superior flavor and marbling.

3. **Poultry Labels**:

    - **Free-Range**: Birds have access to the outdoors, resulting in better flavor.

    - **Organic**: Raised on organic feed without synthetic additives.

    - **Antibiotic-Free**: Raised without the use of antibiotics.

Tips for Selecting Meat:

1. **Marbling**: Look for marbling, the small streaks of fat within the muscle, which provides flavor and tenderness.

2. **Color**: Fresh meat should have a vibrant color—bright red for beef, pinkish-red for pork, and creamy white to yellow for poultry skin.

3. **Packaging**: Ensure the packaging is intact and the meat is cold to the touch, indicating proper storage.

By carefully selecting quality meat and understanding the various cuts and grades, you can elevate your grilling and smoking to new heights. The right meat, combined with your Traeger grill's capabilities, will result in delicious, tender, and flavorful dishes every time.

Preparation Techniques

Proper preparation techniques are vital for maximizing the flavor and texture of your meats and vegetables. Marinating, brining, and seasoning play crucial roles in enhancing taste, while prepping vegetables and sides ensures they complement your main dishes perfectly. Here's how to master these techniques to elevate your grilling experience.

Marinating:

Marinating involves soaking meat in a flavorful liquid mixture, typically composed of an acid (like vinegar or lemon juice), oil, herbs, and spices. The acid helps tenderize the meat, while the oil and seasonings infuse it with flavor. To marinate:

Choose the Right Marinade: Match the marinade to the type of meat. For instance, a citrus-based marinade works well with chicken, while a red wine or soy sauce-based marinade complements beef.

Duration: Marinate meats in the refrigerator. Poultry can marinate for 2-4 hours, beef for 4-8 hours, and tougher cuts like brisket overnight. Avoid over-marinating, as the acid can break down the meat excessively.

Use Resealable Bags or Containers: Ensure the meat is fully submerged and turn occasionally to distribute the marinade evenly.

Brining:

Brining involves soaking meat in a saltwater solution, which helps retain moisture during cooking. Brining is especially beneficial for lean meats like chicken breasts or pork chops. To brine:

Prepare the Brine: Dissolve 1 cup of salt in 1 gallon of water. Add sugar, herbs, and spices if desired.

Soak the Meat: Submerge the meat in the brine and refrigerate. Poultry can brine for 4-6 hours, while pork can brine for 2-4 hours.

Rinse and Dry: Rinse the meat thoroughly after brining to remove excess salt, then pat dry before cooking.

Seasoning:

Seasoning enhances the natural flavors of the meat. Use a blend of salt, pepper, and other spices tailored to your taste preferences. Apply the seasoning generously and rub it into the meat for even coverage.

Prepping Vegetables and Sides:

Vegetables and sides require careful preparation to complement your main dishes. Here are some tips:

Vegetables: Wash and dry vegetables thoroughly. Cut them into uniform sizes for even cooking. Toss with olive oil, salt, and pepper, or marinate them for added flavor.

Skewers: Thread vegetables onto skewers for easy grilling. Alternate colors and textures for visual appeal and balanced cooking.

Foil Packets: Wrap seasoned vegetables in foil packets to lock in moisture and flavors. These are great for grilling alongside meats.

Parboiling: For tougher vegetables like potatoes or carrots, parboil them before grilling to ensure they cook through evenly.

By mastering these preparation techniques, you can ensure that your meats and vegetables are flavorful, tender, and perfectly cooked. These methods enhance the overall grilling experience, resulting in dishes that are not only delicious but also visually appealing and nutritionally balanced.

Chapter 10: Overcoming Common Challenges

Time Management

Grilling can be a time-intensive process, but with proper time management, you can make it an efficient and enjoyable experience even on a busy schedule. Here are some strategies to help you manage your time effectively while grilling:

1. **Plan Ahead**: Preparation is key to efficient grilling. Plan your meals in advance, including the type of meat, vegetables, and sides you'll be cooking. Create a timeline for marinating, brining, and seasoning your ingredients.

2. **Prep in Batches**: Prepare large batches of marinades, rubs, and sauces ahead of time and store them in the refrigerator. This way, you can quickly season your meats and vegetables without the need for extensive preparation each time you grill.

3. **Organize Your Workspace**: Keep your grilling area organized with all the necessary tools and ingredients within reach. This includes having your grill, utensils, meat probes, and cleaning supplies readily available.

4. **Utilize Grill Space Efficiently**: Maximize the use of your grill's cooking surface by planning the placement of different foods. Cook items that require similar temperatures together to avoid frequent adjustments.

5. **Use a Timer**: Set timers for different grilling stages to avoid overcooking or undercooking your food. This is especially useful when grilling multiple items simultaneously.

6. **Multi-Tasking Tips**:

- **Stagger Cooking Times**: Start with items that take the longest to cook, such as large cuts of meat. Once they are well underway, add quicker-cooking items like vegetables or seafood.

- **Prep While Grilling**: Use the downtime while food is grilling to prepare sides, sauces, or salads. This keeps you engaged and efficient.

- **Use Indirect Heat Zones**: For foods that need longer cooking times, use indirect heat zones on your grill. This allows you to cook other items on direct heat simultaneously.

7. **Quick Grilling Options**: Incorporate quick-cooking recipes into your meal plan. Items like burgers, hot dogs, and thin cuts of meat can be grilled in a short amount of time, perfect for busy evenings.

8. **Pre-Cook When Necessary**: For particularly busy days, pre-cook certain components. For example, parboil potatoes or partially cook chicken in the oven, then finish them on the grill for that perfect char and smoky flavor.

By incorporating these time management strategies, you can make grilling a seamless part of your routine, even on the busiest days. Efficient grilling not only saves time but also allows you to enjoy delicious meals without the stress of last-minute preparations.

Safety Tips

Grilling is an enjoyable activity, but it comes with its own set of safety concerns. Following best practices for safe grilling ensures that you can cook without accidents or injuries. Here are some essential safety tips to keep in mind:

1. **Grill Placement**: Always set up your grill in a well-ventilated area, away from any flammable materials, structures, or overhanging branches. Place the grill on a stable, non-flammable surface to prevent tipping.

2. **Proper Lighting**: Use the correct method for lighting your grill. For charcoal grills, use a chimney starter instead of lighter fluid to avoid flare-ups. For gas grills, ensure the lid is open before lighting to prevent gas buildup.

3. **Stay Attentive**: Never leave your grill unattended while in use. Fires can start quickly, and staying nearby allows you to respond immediately to any issues.

4. **Tools and Equipment**: Use long-handled tools designed for grilling to keep your hands and arms safe from the heat. Wear heat-resistant gloves when handling hot grates or adjusting vents.

5. **Control Flare-Ups**: Flare-ups can occur when fat drips onto the heat source. To manage flare-ups, keep a spray bottle filled with water nearby to douse small flames. Move food to a cooler part of the grill if flames get too high.

6. **Proper Ventilation**: Ensure your grill has proper ventilation to prevent the buildup of carbon monoxide, a colorless, odorless gas that can be deadly. Never use a grill indoors or in enclosed spaces like garages.

7. **Handling Propane Safely**: For gas grills, regularly check the propane tank and connections for leaks. Apply a solution of soapy water to the connections and look for bubbles, which indicate a leak. Always store propane tanks upright and outdoors.

8. **Cleanliness**: Keep your grill clean to avoid grease buildup, which can cause flare-ups. Regularly remove grease and food debris from grates, drip trays, and burners.

9. **Fire Extinguisher**: Have a fire extinguisher rated for grease fires readily available. Ensure you know how to use it and that it is in working condition. A bucket of sand can also be useful for extinguishing flames.

10. **Handling Flare-Ups and Emergencies**:

    o **Small Flare-Ups**: Use your spray bottle to control small flare-ups. Close the lid to cut off oxygen and smother the flames if necessary.

    o **Grease Fires**: For larger grease fires, do not use water, as it can spread the fire. Use a fire extinguisher or baking soda to smother the flames.

    o **Burns**: Treat minor burns by running them under cool water for 10-15 minutes. For serious burns, seek medical attention immediately.

    o **Gas Leaks**: If you smell gas while grilling, turn off the grill and propane tank immediately. Do not attempt to relight the grill until the leak is fixed.

11. **Weather Considerations**: Avoid grilling in high winds, which can cause uneven heating and increase the risk of flare-ups. Be cautious when grilling in cold weather; ensure your grill is functioning properly and that you are dressed appropriately to avoid prolonged exposure to cold.

12. **Food Safety**: Always use a meat thermometer to ensure your food is cooked to safe internal temperatures. Keep raw meat separate from cooked foods to prevent cross-contamination. Wash hands, utensils, and surfaces thoroughly after handling raw meat.

By adhering to these safety tips, you can create a secure and enjoyable grilling environment. Being prepared and cautious helps prevent accidents, ensuring that your outdoor cooking experience remains fun and stress-free. Safe grilling practices not only protect you and your loved ones but also contribute to better-cooked, healthier meals.

In conclusion, managing your time efficiently and adhering to safety protocols are crucial aspects of successful grilling. With careful planning, organization, and vigilance, you can enjoy the process and produce delicious, well-prepared dishes without compromising safety. Embrace these best practices to enhance your grilling experience, making it both enjoyable and safe for everyone involved.

26737387R00058